我的友情美文

相遇是一种美丽的缘分

英汉对照 词汇解析 语法讲解 励志语录

马琼琼 编著

中国纺织出版社有限公司

图书在版编目（CIP）数据

我的友情美文：相遇是一种美丽的缘分：汉、英／马琼琼编著. -- 北京：中国纺织出版社有限公司，2019.12（2021.1重印）

ISBN 978-7-5180-6731-2

Ⅰ.①我… Ⅱ.①马… Ⅲ.①英语－汉语－对照读物②散文集－世界 Ⅳ.① H319.4：1

中国版本图书馆 CIP 数据核字（2019）第 219072 号

责任编辑：武洋洋　　责任校对：王花妮
责任设计：晏子茹　　责任印制：储志伟

中国纺织出版社有限公司出版发行
地址：北京市朝阳区百子湾东里 A407 号楼　邮政编码：100124
销售电话：010—67004422　传真：010—87155801
http://www.c-textilep.com
中国纺织出版社天猫旗舰店
官方微博 http://www.weibo.com/2119887771
河北鹏润印刷有限公司印刷　各地新华书店经销
2019 年 12 月第 1 版　2021 年 1 月第 3 次印刷
开本：880 × 1230　1/32　印张：5.5
字数：170 千字　定价：39.80 元

前言

思想结晶改变人生命运，经典美文提高生活品位。曾几何时，一个字，触动你的心弦；一句话，让你泪流满面；一篇短文，让你重拾信心，勇敢面对生活给你的考验。这就是语言的魅力。通过阅读优美的英文短文，不仅能够扩大词汇量，掌握单词的用法，了解语法，学习地道的表达，更让你的心灵如沐春风，得到爱的呵护和情感的滋养。

岁月流转，经典永存。针对英语学习爱好者的需要，编者精心选取了难易适中的英语经典美文，为你提供一场丰富多彩的文学盛宴。本书采用中英文对照的形式，便于读者理解。每篇美文后都附有单词解析、语法知识点、经典名句三大版块，让你在欣赏完一篇美文后，还能扩充词汇量、巩固语法知识、斟酌文中好句，并感悟人生。在一篇篇不同题材风格的英语美文中，你总能找到引起你心灵共鸣的一篇。

读一本新书恰似坠入爱河，是场冒险。你得全身心地投入进去。翻开书页之时，从前言直至封底你或许都知之甚少。但谁又不是呢？字里行间的只言片语不总是正确的。

有时候你会发现，人们自我推销时是一种形象，等你在深入了解后，他们就完全变样了。有时故事的叙述流于表面，朴实的语言，平淡的情节，但阅读过半后，你却发觉这本书真是出乎意料的妙不可言，而这种感受只能靠自己去感悟！

阅读之乐，腹有诗书气自华；阅读之美，活水云影共天光。阅读可以放逐百年孤独，阅读可以触摸千年月光。阅读中有眼前的收获，阅读中也有诗和远方。

让我们静下心来感受英语美文的温度，在英语美文中仔细品味似曾相识的细腻情感，感悟生命和人性的力量。

编者

2019年9月

目录

01 That's What Friends Do (I)
朋友就该这么做（Ⅰ）

Jack tossed the papers on my desk—his eyebrows knit into a straight line as he glared at me.

"What's wrong?" I asked.

He jabbed a finger at the **proposal**. "Next time you want to change anything, ask me first," he said, turning on his heels and leaving me stewing in anger.

How dare he treat me like that, I thought. I had changed one long sentence, and corrected grammar, something I thought I was paid to do.

It's not that I hadn't been warned. Other women who had worked my job before me called Jack names I couldn't repeat. One **coworker** took me aside the first day. "He's personally responsible for two different secretaries leaving the firm," she whispered.

As the weeks went by, I grew to **despise** Jack. His actions made me question much that I believed in, such as turning the other cheek and loving your enemies. Jack quickly slapped a **verbal** insult on any cheek turned his way. I prayed about the situation, but to be honest, I wanted to put Jack in his place, not love him.

杰克把文件扔到我桌上，皱着眉头，气愤地瞪着我。

“怎么了？”我问道。

他指着计划书狠狠地说道：“下次想做什么改动前，先征求一下我的意见。”然后转身走了，留下我一个人在那里生闷气。

他怎么能这样对我！我想，我只是改了一个长句，更正了语法错误，但这都是我的分内之事啊。

其实也有人提醒过我，上一任在我这个职位上工作的女士就曾大骂过他。我第一天上班时，就有同事把我拉到一旁小声说：“已有两个秘书因为他而辞职了。”

几周后，我逐渐有些鄙视杰克了，而这又有悖于我的信条——别人打你左脸，右脸也转过去让他打；爱自己的敌人。但无论怎么做，总会挨杰克的骂。说真的，我很想灭灭他的嚣张气焰，而不是去爱他。我还为此默默祈祷过。

一天，因为一件事，我又被他气哭了。我冲进他的办

One day another of his episodes left me in tears. I stormed into his office, and Jack glanced up. "What?" he asked **abruptly**.

I sat across from him and said calmly, "Jack, the way you've been treating me is wrong. I've never had anyone speak to me that way. As a professional, it's wrong, and I can't allow it to continue."

Jack **snickered** nervously and leaned back in his chair. I closed my eyes briefly. God help me, I prayed.

"I want to make you a promise. I will be a friend," I said. "I will treat you as you deserve to be treated, with respect and kindness. You **deserve** that. Everybody does." I slipped out of the chair and closed the door behind me.

Jack avoided me the rest of the week. Proposals, specs, and letters appeared on my desk while I was at lunch, and my corrected versions were not seen again. I brought cookies to the office one day and left a batch on his desk. Another day I left a note. "Hope your day is going great," it read.

Over the next few weeks, Jack reappeared. He was reserved, but there were no other episodes. Coworkers cornered me in the break room. "Guess you got to Jack," they said. "You must have told him off good."

公室，杰克抬头看了我一眼，“有事吗?”他突然说道。

我在他对面坐下：“杰克，你对待我的方式很有问题。还从没有人像你那样对我说话。作为一个职业人士，你这么做很愚蠢，我无法容忍这样的事情再度发生。”

杰克不安地笑了笑，向后靠靠，我闭了一下眼睛，祈祷着，希望上帝能帮帮我。

“我保证，可以成为你的朋友。你是我的上司，我自然会尊敬你，礼貌待你，这是我应做的。每个人都应得到如此礼遇。”我说着便起身离开，把门关上了。

那个星期余下的几天，杰克一直躲着我。他总趁我吃午饭时，把计划书、技术说明和信件放在我桌上，并且，我修改过的文件不再被打回来。一天，我买了些饼干去办公室，顺便在杰克桌上留了一包。第二天，我又留了一张字条，在上面写道：“祝你今天一切顺利。”

接下来的几个星期，杰克不再躲避我了，但沉默了许多，办公室里再也没发生不愉快的事情。于是，同事们在休息室把我团团围了起来。“听说杰克被你镇住了，”他们说，“你肯定大骂了他一顿。”

I shook my head. "Jack and I are becoming friends." I said in faith. I refused to talk about him. Every time I saw Jack in the hall, I smiled at him. After all, that's what friends do.

我摇了摇头，一字一顿地说："我们会成为朋友。"我根本不想提起杰克，每次在大厅看见他时，我总冲他微笑。毕竟，朋友就该这样。

单词解析 Word Analysis

proposal [prə'pəʊzl] n. 建议，提议

例 The president was in full agreement with the proposal.
总统完全赞同该提议。

coworker ['kəʊˌwɜːkə] n. 同事，同僚

例 I don't like the new male co-worker.
我讨厌那个新来的男同事。

despise [dɪ'spaɪz] v. 蔑视，看不起

例 I can never, ever forgive him. I despise him.
我永远不会原谅他，我鄙视他。

verbal ['vɜːbl] adj. 口头的；文字的

例 They were jostled and subjected to a torrent of verbal abuse.
他们被推来搡去，受到大肆的谩骂攻击。

abruptly [ə'brʌptlɪ] adv. 突然地，意外地

例 He spoke abruptly, in barely comprehensible Arabic.
他突然开口了，说的却是几乎听不懂的阿拉伯语。

snicker ['snɪkə(r)] v. 偷笑，窃窃地笑

例 We all snickered at Mrs. Swenson.
我们都暗暗嘲笑斯温森太太。

deserve [dɪ'zɜːv] v. 应得，应受，值得

例 You deserve a reward for being so helpful.
你帮了这么大的忙，理应受到奖励。

语法知识点 *Grammar Points*

① How dare he treat me like that, I thought.

How dare 怎么敢，dare意为“敢”，其后接动词原形，通常只用于否定句或疑问句以及 if 或 whether 之后，一般不用于肯定句。

例 How dare you say such a thing to me?

你怎么敢对我说这样的话?

I dare say习惯说法（用于肯定句），并不一定要译为“我敢说”，它所表示的是一种不肯定的语气，常译为“大概”“我想”。

例 I dare say you've spent all your money by now.

我估计你现在钱已用完了。

② ...but to be honest, I wanted to put Jack in his place, not love him.

to be honest 老实说

一说到英文里的“说实话”，很多小伙伴们都会想到to be honest或honestly speaking，其实in all honesty意思也是一样的，另外这个短语中的honesty也可以换一换，比如in all seriousness/truthfulness。

例 In all honesty, I do have some criticisms to make.

讲真，我确实有批评意见要提。

类似的还有to tell the truth，to be fair，lay it on the line

例 To tell the truth, I couldn't hear a word he said.

讲真，他说的话我一个字也听不到。

例 To be fair, the team is young and not yet settled.

讲真，这个队伍还很年轻，还不太稳定。

例 Let me lay it on the line: if your work doesn't improve, you'll be fired.

讲真，如果你在工作上没有改进，就等着被炒鱿鱼吧!

③ You must have told him off good.

must have done 一定做过某事。表示对过去事情的较有把握的推测，这时只能用于肯定句中，“肯定/必须已经干过……”，在否定句和疑问句中用can't或couldn't或can/could。

例 The light was out. They must have gone to bed.

灯都熄了，他们一定睡了。

经典名句 *Famous Classics*

1. Success covers a multitude of blunders.
成功由大量的失误铸就。

2. Success often depends upon knowing how long it will take to succeed.
成功常常取决于知道需要多久才能成功。

3. That sort of defeats are only stepping-stones.
那种失败只不过是前进的踏脚石。

4. The greater a man is, the more distasteful is praise and flattery to him.
一个人越伟大，对表扬和奉承就越反感。

5. The human being longs for a sense of being accomplished, of being able to do things, with his hand, with his mind, with his will. Each of us wants to feel he or she has the ability to do something that is meaningful and that serves a tribute to our inherent abilities.
人们渴求有一种成就感，渴望有能力用自己的手、用自己的脑、用自己的意志办事。我们每个人都希望自己能够做出有意义、并能显示出自己天赋的事来。

6. The people who get on in this world are the people who get up and look for circumstances they want, and if they cannot find them, they make them.
在这个世界上，取得成功的人是那些努力寻找他们想要机会的人，如果找不到机会，他们就去创造机会。

02 That's What Friends Do (II) 朋友就该这么做（Ⅱ）

One year after our "talk," I discovered I had breast cancer. I was thirty-two, the mother of three beautiful young children, and scared. The cancer had **metastasized** to my lymph nodes and the statistics were not great for long-term **survival**. After my surgery, friends and loved ones visited and tried to find the right words. No one knew what to say, and many said the wrong things. Others **wept,** and I tried to encourage them. I clung to hope myself.

One day, Jack stood **awkwardly** in the doorway of my small, **darkened** hospital room. I waved him in with a smile. He walked over to my bed and without a word placed a bundle beside me. Inside the package lay several bulbs.

"Tulips," he said.

I grinned, not understanding.

He **shuffled** his feet, then cleared his throat, "If you plant them when you get home, they'll come up next spring. I just wanted you to know that I think you'll be there to see them when they come up."

Tears **clouded** my eyes and I reached out my hand. "Thank you," I

我们的谈话过去一年后，我32岁，是三个漂亮孩子的母亲，但我被确诊为乳腺癌，这让我极端恐惧。癌细胞已经扩散到我的淋巴结。从统计数据来看，我的时间不多了。手术后，亲朋好友来看望我，他们尽量宽慰我，但都不知道说些什么好，有些人反而说错了话，另外一些人则为我难过，还得我去安慰他们。我始终没有放弃希望。

一天，我看到门外有个人影，是杰克，他尴尬地站在门口。我微笑着招呼他进来，他走到我床边，默默地把一包东西放在我旁边，那里边是几个球茎。

"这是郁金香。"他说。

我笑着，不明白他的用意。

他清了清嗓子说，"回家后把它们种下，到明年春天就长出来了。"他挪挪脚，"我希望你知道，你一定看得到它们发芽开花。"

我泪眼蒙眬地伸出手。"谢谢你。"我低声说。杰克抓住我的手，生硬地答道：

whispered. Jack grasped my hand and **gruffly** replied, "You're welcome. You can't see it now, but next spring you'll see the colors I picked out for you. I think you'll like them." He turned and left without another word.

For ten years, I have watched those red-and-white striped tulips push their way through the soil every spring.

In a moment when I prayed for just the right word, a man with very few words said all the right things.

After all, that's what friends do.

"不必客气。到明年长出来后，你就能看到我为你挑的是什么颜色的郁金香了。我想你一定会喜欢。"之后，他没说一句话便转身离开了。

转眼间，十多年过去了，每年春天，我都会看着这些红白相间的郁金香破土而出。

在那绝望的时刻，我祈求他人的安慰，而这个男人寥寥数语，却情真意切，温暖着我脆弱的心。

毕竟，朋友之间就该这么做。

单词解析 *Word Analysis*

metastasize [mɪ'tæstəsaɪz] *v.* 转移

例 Cancer cells metastasize through the body.
癌细胞蔓延全身。

survival [sə'vaɪvl] *n.* 幸存，生存

例 An animal's sense of smell is still crucial to its survival.
动物的嗅觉对其生存仍然至关重要。

weep [wiːp] *v.* 哭泣，流泪

例 The weeping family hugged and comforted each other.
哭泣着的一家人相互拥抱并彼此安慰。

awkwardly ['ɔːkwədlɪ] *adv.* 笨拙地，尴尬地

例 He fell awkwardly and went down in agony clutching his right knee.
他笨拙地摔倒了，痛苦地抱住右膝倒在地上。

darkened ['daːkənd] *adj.* 黑暗的，漆黑的

例 He drove past darkened houses.
他开车经过黑着灯的房子。

shuffle [ˈʃʌfl] *v.* 拖着脚走

例 They shuffled along somewhat reluctantly.
他们有些不情愿地拖着脚走着。

cloud [klaʊd] *v.* 使……朦胧不清

例 I run the water very hot, clouding the mirror.
我把水开得很热，水汽模糊了镜面。

gruffly [grʌflɪ] *adv.* 粗暴地，粗声地

例 When he left he cut short the father's nervous thanks gruffly.
临走时，他很粗鲁地打断了父亲紧张的道谢的话。

语法知识点 *Grammar Points*

① Inside the package lay several bulbs.

这是一个倒装句，为完全倒装，正常语序应为：Several bulbs lay inside the package.

英语中完全倒装主要有四种类型：

表示地点的副词here, there置于句首，且主语是名词（不是代词），需用完全倒装，其形式为：There/Here+谓语+主语。常用于此句型的谓语动词为be, go, come, exist, follow, remain, lie等，时态要用一般现在时。

例 Here is the address of your hotel.
这里就是你宾馆的地址。

表示时间的副词（如：now, then等）、运动方向的副词（如：out, in, up, down, away等）及表示地点的介词短语置于句首，且主语是名词（不是代词），需用完全倒装，其形式为：副词或介词短语+谓语+主语。常用于此句型的谓语动词为come, fall, follow, exist, lie, go, remain, run等，时态为一般现在时或一般过去时。

例 Under the table sleeps a white cat.
桌子下面睡着一只白色的猫。

为了保持句子平衡或强调表语部分等，将作表语的形容词、分词、介词短语、such置于句首时，需使用完全倒装，其形式为：形容词/现在分词/过去分词/介词短语/such+be+主语。

例 Seated on the ground are a group of young people.
席地而坐的是一群年轻人。

② I have watched those red-and-white striped tulips push their way through the soil every spring.

watch是感官动词，英语中感官动词还有see, hear, listen to, notice等词，这些词有共同的用法：后接宾语，再接动词原形或ing形式。前者表全过程，后者表正在进行。句中有频率词时，以上的词也常跟动词原形。

例 I heard someone knocking at the door when I fell asleep.
我入睡时有人正敲门。

例 I often watch my classmates play volleyball after school.
我常常看见我的同学们放学后打排球。

若以上词用于被动语态，后面原有动词原形改为带to的动词不定式。

例 He was seen to go into the restaurant.
他被看见进了饭店。

③ …a man with very few words said all the right things.

with very few words 话特别少

few是否定意义的词，表示“几乎没有”，a few表示肯定，译为“一些，少量的”。

few和a few后面要接可数名词的复数形式；从意义上看，few用来强调小数目的否定意义，相当于说“很少”或“几乎没有”，它的含义是该数目令人失望或令人吃惊得少。

例 Few people like snakes.
很少有人喜欢蛇。

a few的意思与few不同，它没有否定含义，它表示“有几个”，有时甚至还表示“一些”。

例 After a few tries they gave up.
试过几次之后他们就放弃了。

当要与一段时间连用时，我们总是用a few，不用few。

例 We need a place where we can stay for a few days.
我们需要一个能住几天的地方。

经典名句 *Famous Classics*

1. The success is nothing more than doing well whatever you do without a thought of fame.
成功就是好好工作而不计较名利。

2. The world more frequently recommends the appearance of merit than merit itself.
世人往往推崇表面的功绩，而不是推崇真正的功绩。

3. There are two ways of rising in the world, either by your own industry or by the folly of others.
成功之路有两条：靠自己的努力或靠他人的愚蠢。

4. There is only one success—to be able to spend your life in your own way.
成功只有一个——即能依自己的方式去度过人生。

5. To conquer we need to dare, to dare again, ever to dare!
为了胜利，我们需要勇敢，更勇敢！永远勇敢冲杀！

6. To travel hopefully is a better thing than to arrive, and the true success is to labor.
怀着希望去旅行比抵达目的地更愉快；而真正的成功在于工作。

7. Victory won't come to me unless I go to it.
胜利是不会向我走来的，我必须自己走向胜利。

8. Will, work and wait are the pyramidal cornerstones for success.
意志、工作和等待是成功的金字塔的基石。

读书笔记

03 Six Types of Friends You Need (I)
你需要的六种朋友（I）

You need different types of friends in the same way that you need food from different food groups. Different types of friends serve different purposes and nourish and enrich our lives in different ways.While many of us are lucky to count our real friends on one hand, there are certain types of people it's good to have around. So, how many do you know?

你需要不同类型的朋友，就像你需要不同种类的食物一样。不同类型的朋友有不同作用，他们以不同的方式来丰富我们的生活。虽然很多人都很幸运地拥有真正的朋友，但有几种类型的朋友确实值得拥有。那么你知道几种呢?

1. The friend who is cooler than you

1. 比你更酷的朋友

The world changes quickly and some people are just that little bit better at keeping up with what's hip than we are. Like those friends who know that NO ONE EVER says "hip" any more, for instance. We like to be around these people, because they're a beacon of cool. Cool things just flock to them.

这个世界瞬息万变，总有一些人比我们更了解什么是流行，就像有些朋友们知道现在没有人再说“hip”这个词。我们喜欢围绕着这些人，因为他们是流行的指向标。潮流朝着他们蜂拥而至。

These are the people who help you to open your eyes, have a flow-on effect for introducing you to other cool people and help to unstick yourself from the rut that's all too easy to get bogged in. These people enrich your life by exposing you to things that may have otherwise have passed you by.

这些人开阔了你的视野，让你认识到更多的潮人，使我们打破常规，突破自我。他们向你展示一些你可能已经错过的东西，从而丰富我们的生活。

2. The friend who you aspire to be

Oprah Winfrey once said: "Surround yourself with only people who are going to lift you higher." And we all need to live life a little bit closer to Oprah. These people challenge you to be the best version of yourself. The only downside is that sometimes they can be infuriating and inspiring in equal measure. This friend is only an important role model if they behave in ways that are authentic and genuine. They will see the best in you and give you important feedback on both your strengths and weaknesses.

2. 令你渴望成为他那种人的朋友

奥普拉·温弗瑞曾说："和那些可以让你提升自己的人在一起。"我们都需要像奥普拉那样生活，这些人可以激励你变得更优秀，唯一不足的就是，有时候他们激励你的时候又会使你恼羞成怒。如果他们的行为是真诚的，那么他们就是你很重要的行为榜样，他们会看见你最好的一面，也会指出你的优劣。

3. The friend who is painfully honest

An honest friend will not always tell you what you want to hear, but they'll certainly tell you what you need to know like if he/she is really that into you. When you've got a crisis on your hands or need to make a quick decision they are your go-to. They're also there to keep you away from mixing paisleys and stripes.

3. 犀利却诚实的朋友

一个诚实的朋友不会总讲那些你想听的话，但如果他/她是真的关心你，他们会不时地讲一些你想知道的事。在紧要关头或面临进退两难的境地时，他们就是你的首选。他们会让你远离那些麻烦事。

This type of friend has the strength of feedback and is a pearl who will tell it to you straight when others won't or will sugarcoat things at the very least. This friend is someone who does it with good intentions and for your own benefit.

这种朋友有很强的反馈力，他们会直言不讳地告诉你别人不愿说或掩饰的事实。这种朋友这样做是出于好意，是真心为你着想的。

There is something special about this person because they feel like home.

在他们身上有一些特别的东西，让你感觉像家人一样亲

It's nice and comforting to be around someone who has known you forever. This is a friend you never have to put on a brave face for. They know you better than you know yourself and accept you unconditionally.

切。和了解你的人待在一起，会让你感觉很舒服。你不必在他们面前故作坚强，他们比你更了解你自己，而且毫无条件地接受你。

单词解析 *Word Analysis*

nourish ['nʌrɪʃ] v. 给……提供营养，滋养

例 The food she eats nourishes both her and the baby.
她吃的食物给她和婴儿提供了营养。

enrich [ɪn'rɪtʃ] v. 充实，使丰富

例 It is important to enrich the soil prior to planting.
在种植前给土壤增肥很重要。

beacon ['biːkən] n. 灯塔；指引者，楷模

例 He was a beacon of hope for the younger generation.
他是年轻一代的希望之灯。

unstick [ˌʌn'stɪk] v. 使不再粘着，分开

例 Mike shook his head, to unstick his hair from his sweating forehead.
迈克晃了一下头，想把头发从汗涔涔的前额上甩开。

rut [rʌt] n. （人、生活或工作）刻板乏味，一成不变，老一套

例 I don't like being in a rut—I like to keep moving on.
我不喜欢一成不变的生活——我喜欢不断进取。

downside ['daʊnsaɪd] n. 下降，消极面，缺点

例 The downside of this approach is a lack of clear leadership.
这个办法的缺点是没有明确的领导。

infuriating [ɪn'fjʊərieɪtɪŋ] *adj.* 令人大怒的

例 Steve accelerated with infuriating slowness.
史蒂夫令人恼火地缓慢加速。

authentic [ɔː'θentɪk] *adj.* 真的，真实的，真正的

例 She has authentic charm whereas most people simply have nice manners.
她散发出真正的魅力，而大多数人只是举止优雅。

语法知识点 *Grammar Points*

① While many of us are lucky to count our real friends on one hand…

count on 依赖，依靠；期望，指望

例 Doctors could now count on a regular salary.
现在医生们有望获得一份稳定的工资。

例 I can always count on you to cheer me up.
我总是可以依靠你让我振作起来。

count on doing sth. 指望做某事

例 He is counting on winning seats and perhaps a share in the new government.
他指望着能够赢得一些席位，甚至是参与新政府的执政。

② This type of friend has the strength of feedback and is a pearl who will tell it to you straight when others won't or will sugarcoat things at the very least.

at the very least 一点儿，丝毫，至少

例 At the very least, the government must offer some protection to mothers who fear domestic violence.
最起码，政府必须向害怕遭受家庭暴力的母亲们提供某些保护。

at least 至少，尽量（有一种让步的语气在里面）

例 At least this second meeting had helped to thaw the atmosphere.
这第二次会议至少起到了缓和气氛的作用。

经典名句 *Famous Classics*

1. Don't let something that doesn't matter cause you to lose something that does.
别让那些不重要的事影响你，从而让你失去那些真正重要的东西。

2. I never acted out of guilt. I just couldn't live in a world where you don't exist.
我不是因为内疚，我只是无法再继续生活在一个没有你的世界里。

3. Aimless life is like sailing without compass.
漫无目的的生活就像出海航行没有指南针。

4. To overcome the anxiety and frustration of life, you must first learn how to be your own masters.
要克服生活的焦虑和沮丧，得先学会做自己的主人。

5. When a girl tells you about her problems it does not mean that she complains. She trusts you.
当一个女孩向你倾诉她的烦恼，那不是抱怨，那是她对你的信任。

6. If you keep a window open to the past too long, the present can start to get a little chilly.
如果回首往昔的记忆之窗开的时间太长，寒意就会开始侵袭现在的时光。

7. It's easier to fake a smile and act like everything's fine than to have people ask you why.
假装微笑，装作什么都没有发生，要好过别人来问“你怎么了”。

读书笔记

04 Six Types of Friends You Need (II) 你需要的六种朋友（II）

Just like a band or gang of superheroes needs members who have different **talents** and powers, a circle of friends should have exactly the same thing. It's important to have **diversity** and to be able to look for support from a variety of sources. They also help us to keep broader **perspective** on life.

就像一个乐队或是一群超级英雄需要具有不同天赋和能力的成员，一个朋友圈也应这样。拥有差异性并且能够从各种来源中寻求支持很重要，他们也可以帮助我们拥有更广阔的生活视野。

Thus, besides the types of friends mentioned in the last paper, you also need friends as below:

因此，除了上文提到的3个类型的朋友，你也需要下面的几种朋友。

4. The friend who is up for anything

4. 时刻待命的朋友

People are busy, we get it. But there's nothing more frustrating than having to **reschedule** your re-re-re-scheduled catch-up. Everyone needs a friend who you can call at the drop of a hat. A friend who says "Hell yeah, I'm up for that." That's why it's good to have a mate who you don't need to issue a 28-day notice to just to meet for a frappuccino. It's refreshing (the friend, that is, not necessarily the frappuccino.)

我们知道现在每个人都很忙，但最令人沮丧的事是：你不得不一次次重新安排你的行程。每个人都需要一个随叫随到的朋友，他会对你说："嗨，我就来。"我们不需要为了一杯咖啡提前28天预约，这就是拥有这类朋友的好处，这令人感到愉快。（这种朋友不仅可以和你一起喝咖啡，还可以和你一起经历人生。）

This friend is the **flexible**, no **frills** friend who makes your life a breeze. Nothing is ever too hard and they're open to doing new things and changing plans at short notice. Their **enthusiasm**

这种朋友是灵活的，不会摆架子来搅乱你的生活。对他们而言，没有什么事情是不可克服的，他们乐于去尝试做一些新鲜而刺激的事情。他们的热情会感

is **contagious** and you always have more fun when they are around.

染你，当你待在他们身边时你总能收获更多的欢乐。

5. The friend who doesn't know any of your other friends

5. 与你其他朋友不相干的朋友

We like **integration**. We like killing two birds with one stone by catching up with several groups of friends at once. But there are times when you need to make an S.O.S call to a friend who is completely uninvolved and removed from a situation but who can offer objective advice. So it is a bonus that your friendship exists without orbiting around your other ones.

我们喜欢结伴而行，我们喜欢同时交好多朋友以达到一箭多雕的目的，但是有时我们需要一个可以发出“急救信号”的朋友，他与这件事毫不相干，但是可以提供客观的建议。你们的友谊在这个朋友圈之外也可以存在，这是一件令人高兴的事儿。

There is a level of **privacy** to this friendship that doesn't exist in friendship circles. It will be easier to share some of your hopes and dreams, fears and concerns knowing that they are not going to be discussed when you're not around.

这种朋友圈之外的友谊拥有一定程度的隐私，你可以很轻松地倾诉你的希望、梦想、恐惧和担忧，而不用担心你不在场时被别人议论。

6. The friend you've known than you've known yourself

6. 了解你更胜于你了解自己的朋友

History, sometimes it works to your advantage, other times it doesn't. This is that friend who sees you out of the context of your job, your relationship, your other friends and your life as it is now. This is the friend who knew you when you had pimples and a bowl cut.

历史有时候会对我们产生有利的影响，有时候则相反。这些是能看到你的工作背景、人际关系、恋爱关系和现有生活之外的朋友。他们知道你什么时候有过粉刺，什么时候剪过西瓜头发型，他们非常了解你。

单词解析 Word Analysis

talent ['tælənt] *n.* 天资，天赋

例 She is proud that both her children have a talent for music.
她为自己的两个孩子都有音乐天赋而自豪。

diversity [daɪ'vɜːsəti] *n.* 多样化，不同，差异

例 His object is to gather as great a diversity of material as possible.
他的目标就是尽可能多地搜集各种材料。

perspective [pə'spektɪv] *n.* 角度，观点，态度

例 He says the death of his father has given him a new perspective on life.
他说父亲的去世让他对人生有了新的认识。

reschedule [ˌriː'ʃedjuːl] *v.* 重新计划，重新安排

例 Since I'll be away, I'd like to reschedule the meeting.
既然我到时候不在，我想重新安排一下会议的时间。

flexible ['fleksəbl] *adj.* 灵活的，柔韧的

例 Look for software that's flexible enough for a range of abilities.
寻找功能多、适用性强的软件。

frill [frɪl] *n.* 无用的装饰，虚饰

例 This booklet restricts itself to facts without frills.
这本小册子只谈事实，绝无矫饰。

integration [ˌɪntɪ'greɪʃn] *n.* 整合，一体化

例 The aim is to promote closer economic integration.
目的是进一步促进经济一体化。

enthusiasm [ɪn'θjuːziæzəm] *n.* 热情，热忱

例 Their skill, enthusiasm and running has got them in the team.
他们的技术、热忱和跑动能力使他们得以加入这支球队。

contagious [kən'teɪdʒəs] *adj.* 有传染性的，会蔓延的

例 Laughing is contagious.
笑是有感染力的。

privacy ['prɪvəsi] *n.* 隐私，私事

例 He saw the publication of this book as an embarrassing invasion of his privacy.
他觉得这本书的出版侵犯了他的私生活，让他十分难堪。

语法知识点 *Grammar Points*

① …a circle of friends should have exactly the same thing.

a circle of 圈，圈子

例 I have a lot of musician friends so I'm really in a circle of musicians.
我有很多搞音乐的朋友，因此我真的是在音乐人的圈子里。

② Everyone needs a friend who you can call at the drop of a hat.

at the drop of a hat 马上，立刻；一有机会就

例 I love to travel; I'm ready to go at the drop of a hat.
我喜欢旅游，我准备马上就去。

例 He'll start a loud argument at the drop of a hat.
要是你说些什么他不同意的话，他可以马上和你大声争辩。

③ History, sometimes it works to your advantage, other times it doesn't.

to one's advantage 对某人有利

例 The present world situation is to our advantage.
目前的世界形势对我们有利。

例 It will be to your advantage to study abroad.
出国学习将对你有利。

advantage另外两个常见短语有：have the (an) advantage over (of) 优于，比……占有优势；take advantage of 利用（机会、时机、某人弱点等）。

例 You have the advantage over (of) me in experience.
你的经验比我丰富。

例 He always took full advantage of the mistakes made by his rivals.
他总是充分利用对手所犯的错误。

经典名句 *Famous Classics*

1. It is no use crying over spilt milk. We have missed a lot of precious things in our life without knowing to cherish them.
为已经发生的事后悔是没有用的。我们因为不知道珍惜，已经错过许多最宝贵的东西。

2. They who have conquered doubt and fear have conquered failure.
战胜了疑虑和恐惧，就战胜了失败。

3. A goal is not always meant to be reached; it often serves simply as something to aim at.
目标不一定是需要达到的，目标往往只是用来帮助你瞄准方向的。

4. You're throwing away happiness with both hands. And reaching out for something that will never make you happy.
你把自己的幸福拱手相让，去追求一些根本不会让你幸福的东西。

读书笔记

05 The Color of Friendship 友谊的颜色

Once upon a time the colors of the world started to **quarrel**. All claimed that they were the best, the most important, the most useful, the favorite.

从前，世界上的各种颜色进行过一次争吵，每一种颜色都说自己是最好的、最重要的、最有用的和最讨人喜欢的。

Green said: "Clearly I am the most important. I am the sign of life and of hope. I was chosen for grass, trees and leaves. Without me, all animals would die. Look over the countryside and you will see that I am in the **majority**."

绿色说："显然，我是最重要的。我是生命和希望的标志。我被选作青草、树木以及叶子的颜色。没有了我，所有的动物都会死去。展望田野吧，你会看到到处都有我。"

Yellow chuckled: "You are all so serious. I bring laughter, **gaiety**, and warmth into the world. The sun is yellow, the moon is yellow, and the stars are yellow. Every time you look at a sunflower, the whole world starts to smile. Without me there would be no fun."

黄色咯咯地笑出了声，"你们都太严肃了，我给这个世界带来笑声，欢乐和温暖。太阳是黄色的，月亮是黄色的，星星是黄色的，每一次你看到向日葵的时候，整个世界都开始欢笑。没有我就没有快乐。"

Orange started next to blow her **trumpet**: "I am the color of health and strength. I may be scarce, but I am precious for I serve the needs of human life. I carry the most important **vitamins**. Think of carrots, pumpkins, oranges, mangoes, and papayas. I don't hang around all the time, but when I fill the sky at sunrise or sunset, my beauty is so striking that no one gives another thought to any of you."

橙色马上开始自吹自擂："我可是代表健康和力量的颜色。我可能比较稀少，但是我非常宝贵，因为我满足了人们生活的需要。我携带了大多数重要的维生素。想想胡萝卜、南瓜、柑橘、芒果和番木瓜。我并不经常出没在天空，但日出或日落在天际登场时，我的美丽足以惊世，没有人还会想起你们。"

Red couldn't stand it no longer he shouted out: "I am the ruler of all of you. I am blood—life's blood! I am the color of danger and of **bravery**. I am willing to fight for a cause. I bring fire into the blood. Without me, the earth would be as empty as the moon. I am the color of **passion** and of love, the red rose, the poinsettia and the poppy."

红色再也忍不下去了，他喊道："我，是你们所有人的主宰。我是血液——生命的血液！我是危险和勇敢的颜色。我愿意为了一个目标而斗争。我把烈火带入血液。没有了我，地球会像月亮一样变得空虚。我是激情和爱的颜色，是红玫瑰、猩猩木和罂粟。"

Finally Indigo spoke, much more quietly than all the others, but with just as much determination: "Think of me. I am the color of silence. You hardly notice me, but without me you all become **superficial**. I represent thought and reflection, twilight and deep water. You need me for balance and contrast, for prayer and inner peace."

最后，靛青说话了，他的声音比其他人都轻，但却比其他人都斩钉截铁："想想我吧。我是沉默的颜色。你们几乎注意不到我，但是如果没有我，你们全都会变得肤浅。我代表着思想和反省，代表着黎明的微光和深邃的海水。你们需要我来平衡和比较，来祈祷和获求内心的安宁。"

And so the colors went on boasting, each convinced of his or her own superiority. Their quarreling became louder and louder. Suddenly there was a startling flash of bright lightening thunder rolled and boomed. Rain started to pour down **relentlessly**. The colors crouched down in fear, drawing close to one another for comfort.

这样一来，颜色们就不停地自夸，每个人都深信自己无比优越。他们的争吵声越来越大。突然，电闪雷鸣，雨无情地倾盆而下，颜色们惊恐地蜷缩起来，彼此挤在一起挨过这恐怖的时刻。

In the midst of the clamor, rain began to speak: "You foolish colors, fighting amongst yourselves, each trying to dominate the rest. Don't you know that you were each made for a special purpose, unique and different? Join hands

在一片喧嚣声中，雨开始说话了："你们这些愚蠢的颜色，彼此相互争斗，每个人都想支配别人。你们难道就不知道每个人都是天造地设，都是独一无二、彼此不同的吗？携起手来吧。"

with one another and come to me."

Doing as they were told, the colors united and joined hands. The rain continued: "From now on, when it rains, each of you will stretch across the sky in a great bow of color as a reminder that you can all live in peace. The Rainbow is a sign of hope for tomorrow." And so, whenever a good rain washes the world, and a Rainbow appears in the sky, let us remember to appreciate one another.

颜色们按照雨的话，团结在一起，携起手来。雨接着说："从现在开始，每次下雨的时候你们都要变成一个巨大的彩色弓形横跨天空，以证明你们能够和平相处，彩虹就是未来希望的标志。"所以，每当大雨冲刷这个世界时，彩虹都会出现在天空，让我们记住彼此要珍惜。

单词解析 *Word Analysis*

quarrel ['kwɒrəl] *v.&n.* 争吵，吵架

例 I had a terrible quarrel with my other brothers.
我跟其他几个兄弟大吵了一架。

majority [mə'dʒɒrəti] *n.* 多数，大多数

例 The majority of my patients come to me from out of town.
大多数来找我看病的患者都是外省人。

gaiety ['geɪəti] *n.* 高兴，快乐

例 Music rang out, adding to the gaiety and life of the market.
音乐响起来了，给市场增添了一份快乐和生机。

trumpet ['trʌmpɪt] *n.* 小号，喇叭

例 Jones hasn't touched a trumpet in 10 years.
琼斯有10年没吹小号了。

vitamin ['vɪtəmɪn] *n.* 维生素

例 Butter, margarine, and oily fish are all good sources of vitamin D.
黄油、人造黄油和多脂鱼都含有丰富的维生素D。

bravery ['breɪvərɪ] *n.* 勇气

例 He deserves the highest praise for his bravery.
他的英勇行为应该获得最高的赞誉。

passion ['pæʃn] *n.* 激情，热情，热心

例 There was a warmth and passion about him I never knew existed.
他身上有一股我从不知道的热情和激情。

superficial [ˌsuːpə'fɪʃl] *adj.* 表面上的，肤浅的

例 This guy is a superficial yuppie with no intellect whatsoever.
这个家伙是个肤浅的雅皮士，没有什么头脑。

relentlessly [rɪ'lentləslɪ] *adv.* 无情地，残酷地

例 The African sun beat relentlessly down on his aching head.
非洲的太阳无情地照射在他那发痛的头上。

语法知识点 *Grammar Points*

① …but I am precious for I serve the needs of human life.

for (表原因、理由) 因为，由于，置于主句之后，表示非直接的、随后附加说明的理由或推断理由。

例 She didn't go to school, for she was ill.
她没去上学，因为她生病了。

例 It must have rained, for the ground is wet.
一定下过雨，因为地面是湿的。

② …so the colors went on boasting, each convinced of his or her own superiority.

go on doing sth. 继续不停地做某事或间断后继续做原来没有做完的事

例 The students went on talking and laughing all the way.
一路上学生们一直有说有笑。

类似的短语搭配还有go on to do sth.，接着做另一件事。

例 After they had read the text, the students went on to do the exercises.
读完课文后，学生们继续做练习。

③ From now on, when it rains, each of you will stretch across the sky in a great bow of color as a reminder that you can all live in peace.

from now on 从现在起

例 From now on, I won't go to play football at night, I promise.
我发誓从今以后再也不在夜里踢足球了。

例 I won't take any more of your sauce from now on.
从现在开始，我不会再忍受你那些无礼顶撞的话了。

经典名句 *Famous Classics*

1. Everyone should take action with a dream and be strong with a reason. If the heart has no place to perch on, you will always be a drifter no matter where you are.
一个人至少拥有一个梦想，有一个理由去坚强。心若没有栖息的地方，到哪里都是在流浪。

2. A confident man may turn the trivial into the great and the mean into the magic.
有自信心的人，可以化渺小为伟大，化平庸为神奇。

3. We all have moments of desperation. But if we can face them head on, that's when we find out just how strong we really are.
我们都有绝望的时候，只有在勇敢面对的时候，我们才知道我们有多坚强。

4. All you can do is to try your best. Even with those little steps, you're closer to your goal than you were yesterday.
我们能做的只是要拼尽全力，即使迈出的步子再小，我们也比昨天要更接近自己的目标了。

5. Go confidently in the direction of your dreams. Live the life you

have imagined.
朝着梦想的方向自信地走下去，把生活过成你想象的样子。

6. Give everything a shot. You never know what (or who) is going to change your life.
任何事情都应该去尝试一下，因为你无法知道，什么样的事或者什么样的人将会改变你的一生。

读书笔记

06 Friendship—Psyche's Guard 友谊——灵魂的卫兵

Friendship is **indispensable** to people's life. A man without friends is an angel without wings, whose life will suffer in the long tolerance of **loneliness** and **depression**. Friendship is the mother of our **psyche**, who'll warm her kid when hurt occurs. We have much to share with our friends in life, **perplexity**, excitement, bitterness etc. Alas, it's magnificent to maintain a **genuine** friendship.

友谊是人生活中不可缺少的一部分。一个人没有朋友，就如一个天使没有羽翼，长期生活在寂寞与沮丧的折磨之下。友谊是我们的灵魂之母，在孩子遭受创伤时给予她温暖。生活中我们有很多东西需要与朋友分享，困惑、激动、痛苦等。维护一段真正的友谊是多么了不起啊。

It takes many special qualities to make a friend. Understanding should come first. Only when we get a better understanding of each other can we gain an authentic and meaningful friendship. We may find our hobbies of common interests. This feeling of **affinity** gets us closer and closer.

结交朋友需要具备很多专门的品质。首先是理解，只有当我们能更好地理解对方时，我们才能赢得一段真实而有意义的友谊。我们也许会发现共同的兴趣和爱好，这种共鸣能让我们越来越亲密。

It also takes a special kind of love that seems to know no end. Never hesitate to show your **heartfelt** care and kindness to your friend when he/she is in trouble. Love is not selfish. Love is endowed by God that we should treasure all our life.

结交朋友也需要具备一种特殊的似乎无止境的爱。当他/她处于困境时，永远不要犹豫，要向你的朋友表示出由衷的关怀和善意。友谊之爱应该是无私的，是上帝赋予我们的、应当珍视一生的爱。

Tolerance is the third essential part in friendship. We are absolutely

友谊的第三个基本部分是容忍。我们是完全不同的个

different persons. This individual **distinction** may cause conflict between us in every aspect of our life. Don't immerse ourselves in this **infliction** too long. Try to tolerant him/her in an **introspective** mood. Saints are not perfect, let alone those ordinary people like us. Afterwards, we should get a good communication. Never shy to confess.

体，这种个体差异可能会在生活的方方面面给我们带来冲突，不要让自己过多地沉浸在这种伤害之中，试着用一种自我反省的情怀去宽容他/她。圣人也不是无懈可击的，更不用说我们这些普通人，争吵之后，我们应该好好沟通，永远不要羞于忏悔。

Understanding, love and tolerance are the first three essences that come to an authentic friendship. Other qualities are also concerned such as thoughtfulness, trust and patience. Remember, friendship is your psyche's guard, and treasure it.

理解、爱和容忍是一份真正友谊所需的最重要的三个品质，其他品质，如体贴、信任和耐心也非常重要。记住，友谊是灵魂的卫兵，要珍惜它。

单词解析 *Word Analysis*

indispensable [ˌɪndɪˈspensəbl] *adj.* 不可缺少的

例 She was becoming indispensable to him.

她已变得越来越离不开他了。

loneliness [ˈləʊnlɪnəs] *n.* 孤独，寂寞

例 I have so many friends, but deep down, underneath, I have a fear of loneliness.

我虽然有很多朋友，但心底里还是惧怕寂寞。

depression [dɪˈpreʃn] *n.* 抑郁，沮丧，消沉

例 I slid into a depression and became morbidly fascinated with death.

我陷入消沉，开始对死亡有种病态的迷恋。

psyche ['saɪki] n. 灵魂，心智

例 His exploration of the myth brings insight into the American psyche.
他对这个神话的探讨揭示了美国人的心理。

perplexity [pə'pleksəti] n. 困惑，迷惘

例 He began counting them and then, with growing perplexity, counted them a second time.
他开始数，然后更加困惑，于是又数了一遍。

genuine ['dʒenjuɪn] adj. 真正的，名副其实的，非伪造的

例 There was a risk of genuine refugees being returned to Vietnam.
存在将真正的难民遣返回越南的风险。

affinity [ə'fɪnəti] n. 密切关系，亲近

例 He has a close affinity with the landscape he knew when he was growing up.
他对这片从小就了解的土地有着一种归属感。

distinction [dɪ'stɪŋkʃn] n. 区别，差异

例 There are obvious distinctions between the two wine-making areas.
两个酿酒地区之间有着显著的差别。

heartfelt ['hɑːtfelt] adj. 忠诚的，诚挚的

例 My heartfelt sympathy goes out to all the relatives.
我对所有的亲人表示由衷的慰问。

infliction [ɪn'flɪkʃn] n. 痛苦的经历，蒙受

例 Don't immerse yourself in the infliction too long.
不要长时间沉浸在痛苦的经历中。

introspective [ˌɪntrə'spektɪv] adj. 内省的，反省的

例 Satire is a lonely and introspective occupation.
讽刺是一项孤独而又内省的工作。

语法知识点 *Grammar Points*

① It also takes a special kind of love that seems to know no end.

seem to do 好像，似乎，是对事物的主观臆断，表示虚拟，真实情况怎样，并不确定。

例 The maths problem seems to be very difficult to work out.
这道数学题似乎很难解决。

seem后面也可接doing，表示好像。

例 She seemed lacking in enthusiasm when we were talking about that film.
我们谈论那部电影时，她看来好像没多大热情。

② Saints are not perfect, let alone those ordinary people like us.

let alone 更不用说，基本上不用在句首，只用在句中，连接两个句子，有进一步比较之意。

例 There isn't enough room for us, let alone six dogs and a cat.
连我们的地方都不够，更不必说六条狗和一只猫了。

例 He hasn't enough money for food, let alone amusements.
他连温饱都无法解决，就更不用说娱乐了。

除let alone外，“更不用说”在英语中还可用其他一些短语来表达，常见的有not to speak of, not to mention, to say nothing of, much/still/even less, much/still more等。

not to speak of（后接名词）。

例 His friends and colleagues will be very upset, not to speak of his parents.
他的朋友和同事都会为此事难过，更不用说他的父母了。

not to mention或without mentioning（后接名词）。

例 We were served French champagne, not to mention usual cocktail.
他们连法国香槟酒也端来给我们喝，更不用说平常的鸡尾酒了。

to say nothing of（后接名词或动名词）。

例 Many people were badly hurt, to say nothing of damage to the building.

许多人受了重伤，更不用说房屋的毁坏了。

much/still/even less（后接代词、动词或句子）。

例 She can't finish her own work in time, even less help others.
她连自己的工作都不能及时完成，更不用说帮助别人了。

经典名句 *Famous Classics*

1. You can never have too much sky. You can fall asleep and wake up drunk on sky, and sky can keep you safe when you are sad. Here there is too much sadness and not enough sky. Butterflies too are few and so are flowers and most things that are beautiful. Still, we take what we can get and make the best of it.
你永远不能拥有太多的天空。你可以在天空下睡去，醒来又沉醉。在你忧伤的时候，天空会给你安慰。可是忧伤太多，天空不够。蝴蝶也不够，花儿也不够。大多数美的东西都不够。于是，我们取我们所能取，好好地享用。

2. Yesterday is an invalid cheque. Tomorrow is a promissory note and today is the only cash you have.
昨天是一张作废的支票，明天是一张期票，而今天则是你唯一拥有的现金。

3. The world is a book, and those who do not travel read only a page.
世界是一本书，没去旅行过的人，就像是只读了其中一页。

4. Never regret. If it's good, it's wonderful. If it's bad, it's experience.
不必遗憾。若是美好，叫作精彩。若是糟糕，叫作经历。

5. There's no need to rush. If something is meant to be, it will happen, in the right time, with the right person, for the best reason.
无须匆忙，该来的总会来，在对的时间和对的人，因为对的理由。

6. When you have something you really love but it causes you pain, God is just testing you to see if you are strong enough to hold it.
当你真正喜欢一样东西，但它又给你带来伤害的时候，其实这是老天在考验你是否足够坚持。

07 A Great Friendship 伟大的友谊

Thomas Jefferson and James Madison met in 1776. Could it have been any other year? They worked together starting then to **further** the American Revolution and later to shape the new scheme of government. From that work sprang a friendship perhaps **incomparable** in intimacy and the trustfulness of **collaboration** and **indurations**. It lasted 50 years. It included pleasure and **utility** but over and above them, there were shared purpose, a common end and an **enduring** goodness on both sides. Four and a half months before he died, when he was ailing, debt-ridden, and worried about his impoverished family, Jefferson wrote to his longtime friend. His words and Madison's reply remind us that friends are friends until death. They also remind us that sometimes a friendship has a bearing on things larger than the friendship itself, for has there ever been a friendship of greater public **consequence** than this one?

"The friendship which has subsisted between us now half a century, the harmony of our political principles and **pursuits** have been sources of constant happiness to me through that long period.

托马斯·杰斐逊和詹姆斯·麦迪逊相识于1776年。为什么偏偏是这一年呢？当时他们开始共同努力推动美国革命，后来又一同为政府拟订新草案。在这些合作中孕育出的友谊是亲密无间、信诚以托、坚不可摧的。这份友谊维持了五十年，当中包含有欢乐、有协作，他们更志同道合地朝共同的目标迈进，历经多年从不间断地令彼此受益。在离开人世前四个半月时，杰斐逊重病在身，债台高筑，并为家庭的贫困感到忧心如焚，于是他提笔给这位知交好友写了封信。从他的信以及麦迪逊的回复中，我们可以看到：这两个朋友是一生之交；并且有时候，他们之间的友情意义之大更超越了友情本身，这份友谊给大众带来的深远影响是前所未有的。

“你我之间的友谊迄今已经走过了半个世纪，我们在政治原则与追求上取得的协调在过去的漫漫岁月中为我带来了源源不断的快乐。我感到一大

It's also been a great **solace** to me to believe that you're engaged in vindicating to posterity the course that we've pursued for preserving to them, in all their purity, their blessings of self-government, which we had assisted in acquiring for them. If ever the earth has beheld a system of administration conducted with a single and steadfast eye to the general interest and happiness of those committed to it, one which, protected by truth, can never know **reproach**, it is that to which our lives have been devoted. Myself, you have been a pillar of support throughout life. Take care of me when dead and be assured that I shall leave with you my last affections."

A week later Madison replied:

"You cannot look back to the long period of our private friendship and political **harmony** with more affecting recollections than I do. If they are a source of pleasure to you, what aren't they not to be to me? We cannot be deprived of the happy consciousness of the pure devotion to the public good with which we discharge the trust committed to us and I indulge a confidence that sufficient evidence will find its way to another generation to ensure, after we are gone, whatever of justice may be withheld whilst we are here."

安慰的是，我相信你还在兢兢业业地致力于造福子孙后代的事业——这份事业我们曾为他们争取过，我们也努力要把他们透明自治的优良体制流传下去。希望这世界上有一种治理制度，在执行的时候专门有坚定不移的一只眼睛来审视它，监护大众利益和为之奋斗者的幸福，建立在真理基础上的制度将永远与责难无缘，我们一生所致力的也正在这里。我自己，还有你，毕生都为此鼎力支持。请你照顾我的身后之事，也请相信，我的友情永远和你同在。”

一个星期后，麦迪逊写了回信：

“在过去的漫长岁月中，你我的友谊与一致的政治观，总令我在回想时心中无比感动。它们为你带来欢乐，对我又何尝不是如此？我们肩负人民的信任，为大众福利鞠躬尽瘁，从中获得的幸福感是难以泯灭的。我坚信，无论当前对我们的评判怎样，我们的一切贡献，身后的下一代人必将给予公断。”

单词解析 Word Analysis

further ['fɜːðə(r)] v. 促进，推进

例 Education needn't only be about furthering your career.
受教育并不一定只是要推进一个人的事业。

incomparable [ɪn'kɒmprəbl] adj. 极其好的，无与伦比的

例 The views from the house are incomparable.
从房子里向外看到的景色非常优美。

collaboration [kəˌlæbə'reɪʃn] n. 合作，协作

例 There is substantial collaboration with neighbouring departments.
与相邻的一些部门有大量的合作。

induration [ˌɪndjʊ'reɪʃən] n. 硬化，固结

例 The medicine can improve swelling and induration.
该药物能改善水肿和硬化。

utility [juː'tɪləti] n. 功用，效用

例 He inwardly questioned the utility of his work.
他内心质疑自己的工作是否有用。

enduring [ɪn'djʊərɪŋ] adj. 持久的，不朽的

例 Few of them feel bound by any enduring loyalties.
他们中几乎没有人觉得有义务要保持忠诚。

consequence ['kɒnsɪkwəns] n. 结果，后果，影响

例 Wastage was no doubt a necessary consequence of war.
巨大的损耗无疑是战争的必然结果。

pursuit [pə'sjuːt] n. 追赶，追求

例 Relentless in his pursuit of quality, his technical ability was remarkable.
对质量孜孜不倦的追求使他的技能出类拔萃。

solace ['sɒləs] *n.* 安慰，安慰物

例 I found solace in writing when my father died three years ago.
我父亲3年前去世的时候，我从写作中找到了安慰。

reproach [rɪ'prəʊtʃ] *n.* 责备，责骂

例 He looked at her with reproach.
他用责备的目光看着她。

harmony ['hɑːməni] *n.* 融洽，和睦

例 We must try to live in peace and harmony with ourselves and those around us.
我们必须努力和我们自己及周围的人和睦相处。

语法知识点 *Grammar Points*

① ...you're engaged in vindicating to posterity the course that we've pursued for preserving to them.

be engage in (doing) sth. 从事，忙于

例 The European Central Bank is fully engaged in coping with the debt crisis in Europe.
欧洲中央银行忙于处理欧洲债务危机。

例 He was busily engaged in painting the furniture.
他忙于喷涂家具。

② We cannot be deprived of the happy consciousness of the pure devotion to the public good with which we discharge the trust committed to us...

deprive of 剥夺；夺去

例 The failure deprived the physician of his popularity.
失败使那位医生名誉扫地。

例 Many children are deprived of good education simply because they are born in remote villages.
许多孩子没有受到良好的教育，只是因为他们出生在偏僻的乡村。

经典名句 *Famous Classics*

1. The only thing standing between you and your dream is a lot of hard work.
横跨在你和你的梦想之间的唯一东西就是奋力拼搏。

2. The most easily broken thing in the world is the man's wine glass, girls' dream, steel wire-like love, the virtuous of modern society and the holy heart.
这个世界最易碎的就是男人的酒杯、少女的梦想、钢丝般的爱情、现代社会的善良和高贵的心。

3. The reason why people give up so quickly is because they look at how far they still have to go, instead of how far they have come.
人们为什么轻言放弃？因为他们只是看到前方路途遥远，而忘记了身后的一路坚持。

4. There are two powers in the world: one is the sword and the other is the pen. There is a great competition and rivalry between the two. There is a third power stronger than both, that of the women.
世界上最强大的两种东西：一种是剑，一种是笔。这两者之间有很大的竞争性。世界上还有比这两种东西更强大的第三种，那就是女人。

5. Woman must have her freedom, the fundamental freedom of choosing whether or not she will be a mother and how many children she will have. Regardless of what man's attitude may be, that problem is hers—and before it can be his, it is hers alone.
女人必须得有她的自由，最基本的自由是选择是否成为一位母亲以及将生几个孩子。不管男人的态度如何，那都是她自己的事情——也许最后男人也会参与进来，但首先将由她自己做出决定。

6. A wise woman likes but doesn't love, listens but doesn't believe and leaves before she is left.
聪明的女人会喜欢但不会深爱，会倾听但不会相信，会在被抛弃以前先离开。

08 A Forever Friend 永远的朋友

A friend walks in when the rest of the world walks out.

Sometimes in life,

You find a **special** friend;

Someone who changes your life just by being part of it.

Someone who makes you laugh until you can't stop;

Someone who makes you believes that there really is good in the world.

Someone who **convinces** you that there really is an **unlocked** door just waiting for you to open it.

This is Forever Friendship.

When you feel blue,

And the world seems dark and empty,

Your forever friend lifts you up in spirits **and** makes that dark and empty world **suddenly** seem bright and full.

Your forever friend gets you through the hard times, the sad times, and the **confused** times.

If you turn and walk away,

Your **forever** friend follows,

If you lose your way,

Your forever friend guides you and cheers you on.

别人都走开的时候，朋友仍与你在一起。

有时候在生活中，

你会找到一个特别的朋友；

他只是你生活中的一部分，却能改变你整个生活。

他会把你逗得开怀大笑；

他会让你相信人间有真情。

他会让你确信，真的有一扇不加锁的门，在等待着你去开启。

这就是永远的友谊。

当你失意，

当世界变得黯淡与空虚，

你真正的朋友会让你振作起来，原本黯淡、空虚的世界顿时变得明亮和充实。

你真正的朋友会与你一同度过困难、伤心和烦恼的时刻。

你转身走开时，

真正的朋友会紧紧相随，

你迷失方向时，

真正的朋友会引导你，鼓励你。

Your forever friend holds your hand and tells you that everything is going to be okay.

真正的朋友会握着你的手，告诉你一切都会好起来的。

And if you find such a friend, you feel happy and **complete**, because you need not worry.

如果你找到了这样的朋友，你会快乐，觉得人生完整，因为你无须再忧虑。

You have a forever friend for life, and forever has no **end**.

你拥有了一个真正的朋友，永永远远，永无止境。

单词解析 *Word Analysis*

special ['speʃl] adj. 特殊的，专门的

例 A special locking system means the door cannot be opened accidentally.
特殊的锁定系统使门不会被意外打开。

suddenly ['sʌdənli] adv. 突然地

例 Family values are suddenly the name of the game.
家庭价值观突然变得重要起来。

confused [kən'fju:zd] adj. 困惑的，糊涂的

例 Things were happening too quickly and Brian was confused.
事情发生得太快，把布赖恩给弄糊涂了。

convince [kən'vɪns] v. 使相信，说服

例 That weekend in Plattsburgh, he convinced her to go ahead and marry Bud.
在普拉茨堡的那个周末，他说服她嫁给巴德。

unlocked [ˌʌn'lɒkt] adj. 未锁门的

例 He left his house with the door unlocked.
他离开了家，没锁门。

forever [fər'evə(r)] *adv.* 永远，永久

例 It was great fun but we knew it wouldn't go on forever.
这很开心，但是我们知道不会永远这样。

complete [kəm'pliːt] *adj.* 完全的，十足的

例 It shows a complete lack of understanding by management.
这表明管理层对此完全不了解。

end [end] *n.* 最后部分，末尾

例 The report is expected by the end of the year.
预期年底提交报告。

语法知识点 *Grammar Points*

① When you feel blue…

这里的blue不是“蓝色”，而是“忧郁的，沮丧的”。

例 There's no reason for me to feel so blue.
我没有理由感到这么忧郁。

例 It was blue Monday and Henry nodded sleepily over his books.
这是个沉闷的星期一，亨利对着书本打瞌睡。

② Your forever friend lifts you up in spirits.

lift up 激励，鼓舞

例 You lift me up with your love.
你用你的爱激励着我。

lift up 常用作“提起，举起，抬高，吊起”讲。

例 There's no need to lift up your voice; I'm not deaf.
你不必这么高声，我不聋。

例 Don't shuffle, lift up your feet.
别拖着脚走路，把脚抬起来。

③ Your forever friend gets you through the hard times...

get through 度过，熬过（困难或不快的时期）

例 It is hard to see how people get through the winter.
难以想象人们将怎样熬过这个冬天。

除以上外，get through还可表示通过考试；接通；通过（某地、议案等）；用完。

例 I can't get through to Beijing. The line is busy.
我打不通北京的电话，占线。

例 The man was so fat that he couldn't get through the door.
那人胖得连那扇门都过不去。

例 The plan for this term will have to get through the leading group of the school.
本学期计划得经校领导班子通过。

经典名句 *Famous Classics*

1. Behind every successful man there's a lot of unsuccessful years.
每个成功者的背后都有很多不成功的岁月。

2. Life is like riding a bicycle. To keep your balance you must keep moving.
人生就像骑单车，想保持平衡就得往前走。

3. Sometimes you need to be alone, in order to find out who you really are and what you really want.
有时候你需要独处，只为了找到真正的自己和自己真正想要的。

4. Cry when you feel like doing so. There's nothing wrong with crying; cry out all your fear and stress and just face the truth after crying.
想哭就哭。哭没什么不好；把你的害怕和压力发泄出来，只是哭后还要面对现实。

5. If you are passionate about something, pursue it, no matter what anyone else thinks. That's how dreams are achieved.
如果你热爱一样东西，就拼命去追逐它，不管别人怎么看，只有这样梦想才能实现。

6. The worst feeling in the world is knowing you did the best you could, and it still wasn't good enough.
世界上最糟糕的感觉就是，明明知道自己已经做到最好了，但还是不够好。

7. Love does not consist in gazing at each other, but in looking outward together in the same direction.
爱不在于彼此凝视，而在于注视着同一个方向。

8. You know why it's hard to be happy sometimes? Because you find it hard to let go of the things that make you sad.
你知道为什么有时候很难快乐起来吗？因为很难放手那些让你伤心的事物。

读书笔记

09 The Choice of Companion 选择朋友

A good companion is better than a **fortune**, for a fortune cannot purchase those elements of character which make companionship a **blessing**. The best companion is one who is wiser and better than ourselves, for we are inspired by his wisdom and **virtue** to nobler deeds. Greater wisdom and goodness than we possess lifts us higher mentally and morally.

"A man is known by the companion he keeps." It is always true. Companionship of a high order is powerful to develop character. Character makes character in the associations of life faster than anything else. Purity begets **purity**, like begets like; and this fact makes the choice of companion in early life more important even than that of teachers and guardians.

It is true that we cannot always choose all of our companions, some are thrust upon us by business or the social relations of life, we do not choose them, we do not enjoy them; and yet, we have to associate with them more or less. The experience is not altogether without **compensation**, if there be principle

一个好友胜过一笔财富。人性中有一些品质会让友谊变成一种幸福的事，而金钱买不到这些品质。最好的朋友是那些比我们更睿智和更出色的人，他们的智慧和美德会激发我们去做更高尚的事情。他们有着比我们更多的智慧和更高尚的情操，可以在精神上和道德上将我们带入一个新的境界。

"观其友而知其人"，这句话总是对的。高层次的交往会有力地塑造一个人的性情。在交往中，品性对品性的影响胜过其他任何因素。纯洁的品格会培养纯洁的品格，爱好会引发相同的爱好。这些表明，在年少时，选择朋友甚至比选择老师和监护人还要重要。

不可否认，有些朋友总是我们不能选择的。有些是工作和社会关系强加于我们的。我们没有选择他们，也不喜欢他们，可是我们不得不或多或少地与他们交往。不过，只要我们心中有足够的原则来承担压力，与他们交往也并非毫无益处。在大多数情况下，我们还是可以选择

enough in us to bear the strain. Still, in the main, choice of companions can be made, and must be made. It is not best or necessary for a young person to associate with "Tom, Dick, and Harry" without **forethought** or purpose. Some fixed rules about the company he or she keeps must be observed. The subject should be **uttermost** in the thoughts, and canvassed often.

Companionship is education, good or not; it develops manhood or womanhood, high or low; it lifts soul upward or drags it downward; it minister to virtue or vice. There is no half way work about its influence. If it ennobles, it does grandly, if it **demoralizes,** it does it **devilishly**. It saves or destroys lustily. Nothing in the world is surer than this. Sow virtue, and the harvest will be virtue, **Sow** vice, and the harvest will be vice. Good companionships help us to sow virtue; evil companionships help us to sow vice.

朋友的，而且，必须选择。一个年轻人毫无前瞻性，也无目的性地随意与张三李四交往，是不好的，也是没必要的。他必须遵守一些确定的交友原则，应当把它们摆在心中最高的位置，并经常加以审视。

无论是有益的还是有害的友谊，都是一种教导。它可以培育或是高贵，或是卑微的品格；它可以使灵魂升华，也可以使之堕落；它可以滋生美德，也可以催生邪恶；它的影响没有折中之道：如果它让人高尚，就会用一种无比高贵的方式；如果让人堕落，也会用一种无比邪恶的方式。它可以有力地拯救一个人，也可以轻易地毁掉一个人。播种美德，就会收获美德；播种邪恶，就会收获邪恶，这是非常确定的。而有益的友谊帮我们播种美德，有害的友谊则支使我们撒下邪恶的种子。

单词解析 Word Analysis

fortune [ˈfɔːtʃuːn] *n.* 大笔钱，巨款，财富

例 We had to eat out all the time. It ended up costing a fortune.
我们不得不总在外面吃饭，结果花了很多钱。

blessing ['blesɪŋ] n. 幸事，福祉，好事

例 Rivers are a blessing for an agricultural country.
河流对于一个农业国家来说是一种恩赐。

virtue ['vɜːtʃuː] n. 善行，正直的品行

例 Virtue is not confined to the Christian world.
善行并不是仅限于基督教世界。

purity ['pjʊərəti] n. 纯度，纯洁

例 Human life weighed more with him than purity of policy.
人类生命对他而言比政策的纯洁性更重要。

compensation [ˌkɒmpen'seɪʃn] n. 弥补，补偿

例 He received one year's salary as compensation for loss of office.
他得到一年的工资作为失业补偿金。

forethought ['fɔːθɔːt] n. 事先的考虑，深谋远虑

例 With a little forethought many accidents could be avoided.
如果事先稍微多想想，许多事故是可以避免的。

uttermost ['ʌtəməʊst] n. 极端，最大限度

例 If she fled to the uttermost parts of the earth I should pursue her.
任凭她逃到天涯海角，我也要穷追不舍。

demoralize [dɪ'mɒrəlaɪz] v. 使士气低落，使意志消沉

例 Clearly, one of the objectives is to demoralize the enemy troops in any way they can.
很明显，目标之一就是要用一切可能的手段打击敌军的士气。

devilishly ['devəlɪʃli] adv. 过分地，厉害地

例 Flu has a devilishly efficient transmission mechanism.
流感有非常有效的传播机制。

语法知识点 Grammar Points

① Companionship of a high order is powerful to develop character.

of a high order 介词短语做后置定语的用法，在这类定语中有许多是用of引导的。

所有关系：the wealth of the nation 国家的财富
特征：a man of good temper 好脾气的人
动宾关系：love of study 对学习的热爱
主谓关系：the growth of industry 工业的增长
同位关系：the city of Peking 北京城
除了of，还有很多介词可以引起短语作后置定语：
地点：the table near the window 靠窗的桌子
时间：their activities during the holidays 他们假期的活动
特征：the woman with a baby in her arms 那位抱孩子的女人

② …we have to associate with them more or less.

more or less 大约，或多或少，大体上，在句中作状语，可放在修饰词之前，也可放在句末。

例 I hope my advice will be more or less helpful to you.
希望我的建议对你多少有些帮助。

例 The trip will take ten days more or less.
这次旅行约需十天时间。

associate with 与……交往，联系

例 Do not associate with dishonest boys.
不要常和不诚实的孩子在一起。

③ Still, in the main, choice of companions can be made, and must be made.

in the main 基本上，大体上，总的说来

例 In the main, children are taboo in the workplace.
工作场所基本上禁止儿童进入。

例 She has in the main gathered her medical experience from practice.
她主要是从实践中积累了医疗经验。

经典名句 *Famous Classics*

1. What we women need to do, instead of worrying about what we don't have, is just love what we do have.
我们女人需要做的就是，与其担心我们没有的东西，还不如爱我们已经有的东西。

2. God gave women intuition and femininity. Used properly, the combination easily jumbles the brain of any man I've ever met.
上帝给了女人直觉和女人味。使用合理的话，这两者结合就能很容易迷倒我曾遇到过的所有男性。

3. Being a woman is a terribly difficult task, since it consists principally in dealing with men.
做女人难，因为主要是和男人打交道。

4. Women are made to be loved, not understood.
女人生来是被爱的，而不是被理解的。

5. I like being a woman, even in a man's world. After all, men can't wear dresses, but we can wear the pants.
即使是生活在男人的世界里我也喜欢做女人。毕竟，男人不能穿裙子，但是我们能穿裤子。

读书笔记

10 Types of Friends 朋友的种类

A Faraway Friend is someone you grew up with or went to school with or lived in the same town as until one of you moved away. Without a Faraway Friend, you would never get any mail addressed in handwriting. A Faraway Friend calls late at night, invites you to her wedding, always says she is coming to visit but **rarely** shows up. An actual visit from a Faraway Friend is a cause for **celebration** and binges of all kinds. Cigarettes, Chips Ahoy, bottles of tequila.

远方的朋友和你一起长大或上同一所学校，直到其中一位搬走。没有远方的朋友，你可能永远也收不到一封手写的信件。远方的朋友半夜来访、邀请你参加她的婚礼；总是说要来看你，但又很少露面。远方的朋友真的来看你时，那就要庆祝一下，自然要狂欢作乐一番，少不了香烟、土豆片、欢呼声和一瓶瓶的龙舌兰酒。

The Former Friend. A sad thing. At best a **wistful** memory, at worst a dangerous enemy who is in possession of many of your deepest secrets. But what was it that drove you apart? A misunderstanding, a betrayed confidence, an unrepaid loan, an ill-conceived **flirtation**. A poor choice of **spouse** can do in a friendship just like that. Going into business together can be a serious mistake. Time, money, distance, **cult** religions: all noted friendship killers.

啊，过去的朋友，一件令人伤怀的事。最好的能留给你一个情意绵绵的回忆；最糟糕的拥有你许多机密从而成为你危险的敌人。但到底是什么使你们分手的？误解、泄密、未偿还的贷款或恶意的调情。对配偶选择不当也会带来同样的后果。合伙经商可能是一个严重的错误。时间、金钱、距离、邪教都是有名的友谊杀手。

A New Friend is a **tonic** unlike any other. Say you meet her at a party. In your bowling league. At a Japanese

新朋友就像一种与众不同的补品。比如说你在一个晚会上或保龄球俱乐部联合会上遇见了

conversation class, perhaps.

Wherever, whenever, there's that spark of **recognition**. The first time you talk, you can't believe how much you have in common. Suddenly, your life story is interesting again, your insights fresh, your opinion valued. Your various **shortcomings** are as yet completely **invisible**.

她，也许在一个日本会话课上。

随时随地，都会产生撞击的火花。第一次交流的时候，我无法相信你们竟会有如此多的共同话题。刹那间，你的人生经历再次生动起来，你的见解新颖独到，你的观点得到器重，而你的各种缺点却全然不见了。

单词解析 *Word Analysis*

rarely ['reəli] *adv.* 难得地，少见地

例 They battled against other Indian tribes, but rarely fought with the whites.

他们同其他印第安部落作战，但很少与白人并肩对敌。

celebration [ˌselɪ'breɪʃn] *n.* 庆祝，活动，庆典

例 I can tell you, there was a celebration in our house that night.

告诉你，那天晚上我家开了个庆祝会。

wistful ['wɪstfl] *adj.* 渴望的，伤感的，惆怅的

例 I can't help feeling slightly wistful about the perks I'm giving up.

我不禁对自己将要放弃的津贴感到有点儿不舍。

flirtation [flɜː'teɪʃn] *n.* 调情，调戏，挑逗

例 A casual flirtation could turn into something far more serious around that time.

当时，一个无心的挑逗都可能造成非常严重的后果。

spouse [spaʊs] *n.* 配偶

例 A friend betrays us; a parent abuses us; a spouse leaves us.

会有朋友的背叛，会有父母的错怪，会有配偶的弃离。

cult [kʌlt] *adj.* 受特定群体欢迎的，作为偶像崇拜的

例 Since her death, she has become a cult figure.
她死后成了部分人狂热崇拜的偶像。

tonic ['tɒnɪk] *n.* 有兴奋(或激励)作用的事物

例 Seeing Marcus at that moment was a great tonic.
在那一刻见到马库斯是非常令人兴奋的事。

recognition [ˌrekəg'nɪʃn] *n.* 认知

例 He searched for a sign of recognition on her face, but there was none.
他试图在她的脸上找出一丝认出他的神情，但是根本没有。

shortcoming ['ʃɔːtkʌmɪŋ] *n.* 缺点，短处

例 Marriages usually break down as a result of the shortcomings of both partners.
婚姻常因为配偶双方的缺点而破裂。

invisible [ɪn'vɪzəbl] *adj.* 看不见的

例 Some stars are invisible to the naked eye.
有些星体肉眼是看不见的。

语法知识点 *Grammar Points*

① …at worst a dangerous enemy who is in possession of many of your deepest secrets.

at worst 在最坏的情况下

例 Don't worry about your driving test. At worst you'll fail, and then you can always take it again.
别担心你的驾驶考试，最坏的可能就是没通过，然而你总可以随时再考。

in possession of是介词短语。其主语通常是"占有者"或"拥有者"（通常指"人"），其宾语通常为"被占有或拥有的物体"，意为"拥有/占有……"。

例 Who is in possession of the store?
这家店铺是谁的?

in the possession of 的主语通常为“被占有的东西”，宾语则是某个东西的拥有者。（刚好和前一个相反），在翻译时，in the possession of 通常被翻译成为“……被占有”或“……在……手中”。

例 The Chevorlet is in the possession of the old man.
这辆雪弗莱轿车是属于这位老人的。

② The first time you talk, you can't believe how much you have in common.

have...in common 在……方面有共同之处，后面通常加with，表示“和……有共同之处”。

have a lot (much)/something/little/nothing in common 有很多/一些/几乎没有/没有相同之处

例 We have a lot in common with each other; so we have become good friends.
我们有许多共同之处，所以我们成了好朋友。

例 My views have much in common with yours.
我们俩的观点有许多共同之处。

经典名句 *Famous Classics*

1. Do you understand the feeling of missing someone? It is just like that you will spend a long hard time to turn the ice-cold water you have drunk into tears.
你知道思念一个人的滋味吗？就像喝了一大杯冰水，然后用很长很长的时间流成热泪。

2. A life, a fulfilling life, a rich life includes ups and downs, includes pain and getting up again, includes failure and getting up again.
生活，令人满意的生活，丰富的生活包括了起起落落，包括了痛苦和再次振作，包括了失败和再次奋斗。

3. You'll be amazed at how high you can fly when you leave some of the baggage behind!
丢下一些包袱后，你会惊讶到，自己竟能飞得那么高。

4. In three words I can sum up everything I've learned about life: it

goes on.
我对生活的感悟可以用这几个字来概括：一切都会过去的。

5. Life is what happens to you while you're busy making other plans.
生活总是计划赶不上变化。

6. From your parents you learn love and laughter and how to put one foot before the other; but when books are opened you discover that you have wings.
你从父母那里学到爱、学到笑、学到怎么走路。可是一打开书，你会发现你有了翅膀。

7. Laziness is like a lock, which bolts you out of the storehouse of information and makes you an intellectual starveling.
懒惰就像一把锁，锁住了知识的仓库，使你的智力变得匮乏。

8. Education is the ability to listen to almost anything without losing your temper or self confidence.
教育就是要使人具备一种能力，可以听到任何话都不动怒或丧失自信。

读书笔记

11 Friendship in China and West (I)
中西方友谊（Ⅰ）

Chinese expect friendships to be more **lasting**.

中国人希望友谊天长地久。

For Chinese a true friendship **endures** throughout life changes. Chinese are friends even if they haven't spoken for 20 years.

对于中国人而言，真正的友谊可以经得住生活变故的考验。即使有20年都没能说话，那也是朋友。

If you shared something at one time, then all your life you are friends.

如果你曾经和朋友们分享过快乐，那么你们会是一辈子的朋友。

This is the best of Guanxi, the Wide Web that connects Chinese through time and space.

这是一种最好的关系，互联网让中式友谊没有时空的限制。

Chinese invented the Internet long before Bill Gates was born.

在比尔·盖茨出生前，中国人就发明了网络。

In North America, even the **relationship** in which people feel close and tell each other **personal** problems may not **survive** life changes such as moving to another city, graduation from a university, a change in **economic** circumstances, or marriage.

在北美，即使之前关系亲密无间的朋友，也可能会因为搬家到另一个城市，从大学毕业，家庭经济状况发生变化，或者是结婚而终止了友谊。

If the people do not see each other regularly, the relationship is likely to die.

如果人们不能经常看到对方，那么朋友关系也可能会消失。

Different **foundations** for friendships Chinese friends share "things in common": a task, a class, the hometown.

友谊的建立有不同的基础，其中的共同点是：同一个任务，同一个班级，同一个家乡。

Friendships are formed by people who work or go to school together.

友谊建立在那些一起工作或者一起上学的伙伴之间。

You may or may not like the person, but if he or she can do something for

你可能喜欢或者不喜欢某个人，但是如果他或者她能够凭

you because of his **position** or job, you can be friends.

借自己的职位和工作为你做一些事，那么你们也可以是朋友。

But in North America, business and friendship are kept **separate**. The friendships are usually tied to **specific** activities.

但是在北美，生意和友谊是分开的。友谊通常是和某个特别的活动有关系。

A person may have work friends and leisure activity friends.

一个人也许有工作朋友，或者娱乐活动的朋友。

Also friends tend to have similar financial circumstances, because friendship in the west is based on **equality**.

当然，朋友们间的经济水平也在同一水平上，因为西方的友谊是建立在平等的基础上的。

Friends should exchange similar activities and give similar things to each other.

朋友间应该能够参与彼此的活动，给予对方类似的东西。

单词解析 *Word Analysis*

lasting ['lɑːstɪŋ] *adj.* 持久的，恒久的

例 We are well on our way to a lasting peace.
我们已在实现持久和平上取得很大进展。

endure [ɪn'djʊə(r)] *v.* 容忍，忍耐

例 The company endured heavy financial losses.
那家公司遭受了严重亏损。

relationship [rɪ'leɪʃnʃɪp] *n.* 关系，关联

例 There is a relationship between diet and cancer.
饮食结构和癌症之间有一定关联。

personal ['pɜːsənl] *adj.* 个人的，私人的

例 He learned this lesson the hard way—from his own personal experience.
他这个教训来之不易——是从他自己的亲身经历中得来的。

survive [sə'vaɪv] v. 幸存，存活

例 Those organisms that are most suited to the environment will be those that will survive.

最适宜该环境的微生物将会存活下来。

economic [ˌiːkə'nɒmɪk] adj. 经济的，经济上的

例 The pace of economic growth is picking up.

经济增长的步伐正在加快。

foundation [faʊn'deɪʃn] n. 基础，根基

例 The issue strikes at the very foundation of our community.

这个问题严重影响了我们社会的基本根基。

position [pə'zɪʃn] n. 身份，地位

例 The boss retains enormous influence by reason of his position.

老板由于自身的地位而一直有极大的影响力。

separate ['seprət] adj. 分开的，单独的

例 Each villa has a separate sitting-room.

每栋别墅都有一间独立的起居室。

specific [spə'sɪfɪk] adj. 特定的，指定的

例 There are several specific problems to be dealt with.

有几个特定的问题需要解决。

equality [i'kwɒləti] n. 同等，平等

例 There are no all-embracing EC directives on race equality.

关于种族平等，欧盟指令也无法面面俱到。

语法知识点 *Grammar Points*

① Chinese invented the Internet long before Bill Gates was born.

long before 在……的很久以前，在还没有……的很久以前

例 He had worked in the factory long before he got married.

在他结婚以前，他就在这家工厂工作很长时间了。

此时的主句谓语通常用过去完成时，但有时也可用一般过去时（因为before已体现了动作的先后关系）。

例 This happened long before you were born.
这事在你还没出生以前很久就发生了。

long before也可单独使用，表示比过去某时早得多的时间，译为“老早，早就”。

例 That had happened long before.
那事老早就发生了。

long before 的其他用法：It is（was, will be）long before… 在……前需要很久

例 It was long before he came back.
过了好久他才回来。

例 It won't be long before we see each other.
不久我们又会见面的。

类似词组：before long 不久，很快。

例 Before long he got married.
不久他就结婚了。

② If the people do not see each other regularly, the relationship is likely to die.

be likely to 可能的，要发生的，有……倾向的

例 But the boss said we were likely to work overtime today.
但是老板说我们今天很可能要加班。

例 Noticing that there was likely to be trouble, they sneaked away.
他们看到有可能发生麻烦，就悄悄离开了。

经典名句 *Famous Classics*

1. At twenty years of age, the will reigns; at thirty, the wit; and at forty, the judgment.
二十岁时起支配作用的是意志，三十岁时是机智，四十岁时是判断。

2. The first wealth is health.
健康是人生的第一财富。

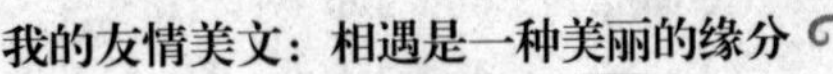

3. A strong man will struggle with the storms of fate.
强者能同命运的风暴抗争。

4. Until you make peace with who you are, you'll never be content with what you have.
除非你能和真实的自己和平相处，否则你永远不会对已拥有的东西感到满足。

5. Behind every successful man there's a lot of unsuccessful years.
每个成功者的背后都有很多不成功的岁月。

6. If you would go up high, then use your own legs! Do not let yourselves carried aloft; do not seat yourselves on other people's backs and heads.
如果你想走向高处，就要使用自己的两条腿！不要让别人把你抬到高处；不要坐在别人的背上和头上。

7. The dictionary is the only place where success comes before work.
只有在字典中，成功才会出现在工作之前。

8. What makes life dreary is the want of motive.
没有了目的，生活便会郁闷无光。

读书笔记

12 Friendship in China and West (II) 中西方友谊（Ⅱ）

If one can **afford** to treat the other to a meal at an expensive restaurant and the other does not have enough money to do the same, it will cause problems in the relationship.

如果一个人能够支付起请朋友去昂贵餐厅吃饭的费用，而另一个人却没有足够的钱回请，那么这样的友谊会产生问题。

Westerns expect friends to be **independent.**

西方人希望朋友间是相互独立的。

Western people prefer people to be independent, so they do not feel comfortable in a relationship in which one person is giving more and the other **is dependent on** what is giving.

因为有了这样的独立意识，对于朋友间一方给予多，另一方难以对等给予的这种关系，他们觉得这种友谊会令人不舒服。

Their friendship is **mostly** a matter of providing **emotional** support and spending time together.

他们的友谊更多意味着相互给予对方精神上的支持，一起度过一段时间。

A westerner will respond to a friend's trouble by asking "What do you want to do?"

一个西方人在回应朋友的求助时，常会问："你想怎么做？"

The idea is to help the friend to think out the problem and discover the **solution** he or she really wants and then to support the solution.

帮助朋友的办法是思考问题，寻求他/她确实需要的解决办法，并且支持对方那么去做。

Chinese friends give each other more **concrete** help. A Chinese will use personal **connections** to help a friend get something hard to obtain such as a job, or an appointment with a good doctor.

中国人给予朋友更多具体的帮助。他/她可能会利用自己的关系帮助朋友取得不容易得到的东西，比如一份工作，约见一位好医生。

Chinese friends give each other

中国人可能会在经济上给

money and might help each other out **financially** over a long time.

予相互的帮助，比如给对方金钱帮助他/她渡过难关。

Chinese usually expect more from their friends.

中国人期望得到朋友更多的帮助。

In the West, you can certainly ask friend to do something with you, but you recognize that your friend may say no, if he/she gives you a reason.

在西方，你可以问朋友是否可以为你做点什么，但是你会发现他们可能会说不，他/她可能会给你一个理由。

You would not expect a friend to drop everything to respond to a **non-urgent** need such as shopping.

你不会指望一个朋友放下手头的事情陪你做些不要紧的事情，比如购物。

Nor would you expect a friend to recognize and respond to your wishes without stating them.

也不会期待在你没有跟他们表明的情况下，了解和回应你的愿望。

A friend in China is someone who offers help without waiting to be asked. There are few limits to what you can expect from a friend.

一个中国朋友当你遇到困难时，会主动伸出援助之手。你对朋友期望的限制很少。

You can feel free to tell your friend what he/she can or should do to help or please you.

你可以随时告诉你的朋友他或者她应该怎么来帮助你或者让你高兴。

单词解析 Word Analysis

afford [ə'fɔːd] v. 负担得起

例 My parents can't even afford a new refrigerator.

我父母甚至买不起一台新冰箱。

independent [ˌɪndɪ'pendənt] adj. 相互独立的，彼此不关联的

例 She would like to be financially independent.

她希望在经济上能够自立。

mostly ['məʊstli] adv. 多半，主要

例 I am working with mostly highly motivated people.
和我共事的人大多积极性极高。

emotional [ɪ'məʊʃənl] adj. 情感上的

例 Victims are left with emotional problems that can last for life.
受害者心中留下了可能会持续一生的情感创伤。

solution [sə'luːʃn] n.（问题、困难等的）解决办法

例 He has sought to find a peaceful solution.
他试图寻求和平解决。

concrete ['kɒŋkriːt] adj. 具体的，确凿的

例 There were no concrete proposals on the table.
没有具体的提议可供讨论。

connection [kə'nekʃn] n. 关系，联系

例 The police say he had no connection with the security forces.
警方说他与安全部队没有关系。

financially [fə'nænʃəlɪ] adv. 财政上，经济上

例 Life for the successful doctor can be emotionally and financially rewarding.
对于事业有成的医生来说，精神和物质生活两方面都能令人满足。

语法知识点 *Grammar Points*

① Western people prefer people to be independent…

prefer sb. to do 希望/宁愿某人能够做某事

例 They preferred their son to go to college.
他们希望儿子能够上大学。

prefer表示“宁愿”的意思是，常用的短语还有prefer to do rather than do sth. 表示“宁愿……而不愿意……”，rather than 可用instead of 替代，后面的不定式通常省略to，但前面的不定式必须带to。

例 He preferred to die rather than (to) steal.

他宁死也不去偷窃。

在现代英语中，prefer...rather than...也可用于连接两个名词或动名词，此时的rather than也可换成介词to。

例 I prefer swimming rather than cycling.

比起骑自行车来我还是喜欢游泳。

prefer还可表示“更喜欢”，常用固定搭配prefer...to...，主要用于比较两个名词或动名词。

例 I prefer the seaside to the mountains.

我喜欢海边，不喜欢山区。

例 Tom prefers reading to talking.

汤姆喜欢读书而不喜欢聊天。

② There are few limits to what you can expect from a friend.

expect from 期望（某人）会做出（某事）

例 The standard of your work has fallen from the level we expect from you.

你的工作质量没有达到我们期望的水平。

经典名句 *Famous Classics*

1. Accept what was and what is, and you'll have more positive energy to pursue what will be.

接受过去和现在的模样，才会有能量去追寻自己的未来。

2. A contented mind is the greatest blessing a man can enjoy in this world.

知足是人生在世最大的幸事。

3. Enrich your life today; yesterday is history. Tomorrow is mystery.

充实今朝，昨日已成过去，明天充满神奇。

4. Great works are performed not by strength, but by perseverance.

完成伟大的事业不在于体力，而在于坚韧不拔的毅力。

5. The wealth of the mind is the only wealth.

精神的财富是唯一的财富。

6. Shallow men believe in luck. Self-trust is the first secret of success.
肤浅的人相信运气，而成功的第一秘诀是自信。

7. We always like those who admire us; we do not always like those whom we admire.
我们总是喜欢崇敬我们的人，但并不永远喜欢我们所崇敬的人。

8. If a man deceives me once, shame on him; if twice, shame on me.
人欺我一次，此人可耻；欺我二次，我可耻。

读书笔记

13 We Need Friends 我们需要朋友

The word, friend, covers a wide range of meanings. It can be a nodding **acquaintance**, a comrade, a confidant, a partner, a playmate, an **intimate** colleague, etc.

“朋友”这个词的意义很广。朋友可以是点头之交、同志、知己、伙伴、玩伴、亲密的同事等。

Everyone needs friendship. No one can sail the ocean of life single-handed. We need help from, and also give help to, others. In modern society, people attach more importance to relations and connections. A man of charisma has many friends. His power lies in his ability to give.

人人都需要友谊，没有人能独自在人生的海洋中航行。我们给人以帮助，也需要别人的帮助。在现代社会，人们更重视关系和联系。一个有非凡魅力的人有许多朋友，他的力量在于他的奉献能力。

As life is full of **strife** and **conflict**, we need friends to support and help us out of difficulties. Our friends give us warnings against danger. Our friends offer us advice with regard to how to deal with various situations. True friends share not only our joys but also our sorrows.

生活充满矛盾和斗争，我们需要朋友的支持，以帮助我们摆脱困境。朋友提醒我们警惕险滩。朋友主动给我们以忠告，告诉我们如何应付各种不同的局势。真正的朋友会与我们同甘共苦。

With friendship, life is happy and **harmonious**. Without friendship, life is sad and **unfortunate**. I have friends in high positions and friends in the rank and file. Some are rich and in power. Some are **relatively** poor and without power. Some are like myself, working as

有了友谊，生活幸福、和谐；没有友谊，生活变得悲伤、不幸。我有地位高的朋友，也有地位低的朋友；有的有钱有权，有的较穷且无权无势。有的和我一样教书，读读写写，满足于简朴的生活。我

a teacher, reading and writing, content with a simple life. We all care for each other, love and help each other. We feel we are happiest when we chat and exchange ideas with one another. With my friends, I know what to treasure, what to **tolerate** and what to share.

们都互相关心，互相爱护，互相帮助。我们觉得朋友们在一起闲谈交流思想时最开心。对我的朋友们，我知道该珍惜什么，容忍什么，分享什么。

I will never forget my old friends, and I'll keep making new friends. I will not be cold and **indifferent** to my poor friends, and I will show concern for them, even if it is only a comforting word.

我决不会忘记老朋友，同时继续结交新朋友。我对穷朋友绝不冷漠，而是关心他们，哪怕只是一句安慰的话。

单词解析 *Word Analysis*

acquaintance [ə'kweɪntəns] n. 认识的人，泛泛之交

例 I have a large circle of friends and acquaintances engaged in photography.
我在摄影界交游甚广。

intimate ['ɪntɪmət] adj. 亲密的，密切的

例 I discussed with my intimate friends whether I would immediately have a baby.
我与密友们讨论我是否要马上生孩子。

strife [straɪf] n. 严重不和，冲突

例 Money is a major cause of strife in many marriages.
金钱是造成很多婚姻不和的一个主要原因。

conflict ['kɒnflɪkt] n. 争执，争辩，分歧

例 Try to keep any conflict between you and your ex-partner to a minimum.
尽量将自己与前配偶之间的摩擦减到最小。

harmonious [hɑːˈməʊniəs] *adj.* 和谐的，融洽的

例 Their harmonious relationship resulted in part from their similar goals.

他们关系融洽的部分原因是他们有着相似的目标。

unfortunate [ʌnˈfɔːtʃənət] *adj.* 不幸的，倒霉的

例 Some unfortunate person passing below could all too easily be seriously injured.

从下面经过的倒霉蛋儿很容易受重伤。

relatively [ˈrelətɪvli] *adv.* 相对地，相比较地

例 The sums needed are relatively small.

需要的金额相对较小。

tolerate [ˈtɒləreɪt] *v.* 容忍，忍耐

例 She can no longer tolerate the position that she's in.

她再也受不了自己的处境了。

indifferent [ɪnˈdɪfrənt] *adj.* 漠不关心的，冷淡的

例 People have become indifferent to the suffering of others.

人们对别人的痛苦已经变得无动于衷。

语法知识点 *Grammar Points*

① …people attach more importance to relations and connections.

attach more importance to 更重视（后面加名词，代词或动名词）

例 For such a big sum, we should attach importance to it.

数目如此之大，我们将予以重视。

例 More and more people attach importance to reducing greenhouse gas emission.

越来越多的人开始重视减少温室气体排放。

② Our friends offer us advice with regard to how to deal with various situations.

with regard to 关于，这个句型的标准形式是“With regard to+主语+谓语+其他成分”，当然有时候也是可以放在句子中间部分的，它可翻译为“关于”“至于”“就……而言”。

例 With regard to hardness, the diamond is in a class by itself.
讲硬度，金刚钻是独一无二的。

例 I think, with regard to Maria, her situation is a very delicate one.
我想，就玛丽亚而言，她的情况也非常令人操心。

与这个句型用法相似的句型是“in regard to+主语+谓语+其他成分”。

例 In regard to your request for information, I regret to inform you that I am unable to help you.
关于你需要情报的事，我遗憾地告诉你我没法帮助你。

③ Some are like myself, working as a teacher, reading and writing, content with a simple life. We all care for each other.

be like 像……一样，用于问话时，询问某人的外表、品行或某物的情况，在陈述句中表示说话人的判断。

例 He is just like everybody else.
他和别人完全一样。

类似词组look like，用于问话时，询问答话者认为某人或某物像什么，在陈述句中表示说话人认为他或它像什么。

例 What does he look like?
他看起来像是什么样的人?

content with 满足，满意

例 He professed to be content with the arrangement.
他声称自己对这个安排满意。

care for 照顾，喜欢；介意

例 The sick child was well cared for night and day.
那个生病的孩子日夜受到很好的看护。

例 It seemed to be her mission to care for her brother’s children.
照顾她兄弟的孩子似乎成了她一生的使命。

经典名句 *Famous Classics*

1. What you don't start today won't be finished by tomorrow.
你今天不开始行动，明天怎么可能完成呢。

2. If you're waiting for the perfect conditions, ideas or plans to get started, you'll never achieve anything.
如果你要等有了完美的条件、想法或计划才开始行动，那你会一事无成。

3. You cannot change what you refuse to confront.
不去面对，何谈改变。

4. To be successful does not mean you have to dominate others; it means you have to dominate your own potential.
成功不意味着你要掌控别人，而是要掌控你自己的潜能。

5. Your success isn't just about you. It's about how you positively impact the lives around you.
你的成功不仅仅与你个人有关，它意味着你要给你周围的人带去积极的影响。

6. Being busy and being productive are two different things.
忙忙碌碌和工作高效是完全不同的两码事。

7. There's no such thing as "risk free". Everything you do or don't do has an inherent risk.
世界上没有不存在风险的事。每件事都有其内在的风险，无论你做或者不做。

8. No matter how smart you are, you will make mistakes.
智者千虑，必有一失。

读书笔记

14 Platonic Friendship 柏拉图式友谊

It's a Friday night. Your girl friends are out at a bar and your boyfriend is playing soccer with his mates. Two text messages later, you're eating pizza and watching action movies with three guy friends. Perfect.

"Guy friends" have the **potential** to enrich your life in ways that female friends and boyfriends just can't. For starters, they provide an insider's perspective on how men think, feel and behave. When dealing with male relatives, coworkers and even boyfriends, another man's point of view can be incredibly useful. Three hours spent analyzing a situation in a café with your girlfriends can't compete with a quick chat to a guy friend.

"I love getting an **alternative** perspective from guy friends," says Nellie Gaintsev, 22, an Interior Design student at The University of Technology, Sydney. "In particular, when I'm arguing with my boyfriend, my close guy friends provide me with an understanding of where he may be coming from."

Many women find that time spent with male friends can be a liberating

正值周五晚上，你的闺蜜都去酒吧了，男友也和同伴们踢足球去了。两条短信过后，你就已经和三位男闺蜜一起边吃披萨，边看动作片了，这真是棒极了。

与你的女性朋友和男友不同，“男闺蜜”可以通过另外一些方式来让你的生活变得更加多彩。首先，他们可以就男性的想法、感受以及行为给出一些内部人士的观点。在处理与男性亲属、同事，甚至另一半之间的关系时，另一位男性的观点会极其奏效。与其花三个小时同闺蜜坐在咖啡馆中一起分析状况，不如同男闺蜜的一次快速交谈。

22岁的奈丽是悉尼科技大学室内设计专业的一名学生，她说：“我很喜欢从男性闺蜜那里得到一种全新的观点，尤其是在同男友吵架时，男闺蜜们能站在男性的角度告诉我男友是怎么想的。”

很多女性发现，花时间同男性友人相处，可以说是与女性朋友相处之后的一种释放，

and **somewhat** refreshing break from spending time with the girls. Without the **judgmental** gaze of other females, there is less **pressure** to dress up and compete for attention.

或者某种程度上是一次放松身心的休闲时光，因为少了其他女伴的那种主观的评判目光，你不必为穿着打扮和争抢风头而劳神。

"I think guy friends are a lot more laid back and easy going," says Johanna Gibson, 22, a media student at the University of Sydney. "I find they're more **protective** and generally look out for you in the same way that an older brother would."

就读于悉尼大学传媒专业，22岁的乔娜·吉普森说："我觉得男性朋友要随和得多，我发现他们更具有保护欲，会像大哥哥那样照顾你。"

Traditionally, girl-guy friendships are seen as hard to maintain. Most relationships between males and females that we come across in our day-to-day lives, whether in movies or books, are romantic by nature. These cultural images make girl-guy friendships seem impossible.

长久以来，人们都认为男女间的友谊很难维持。在书籍或电影中，我们日常生活中所遇到的大多数男女关系都会自然而然产生化学反应，这些文化意象让人觉男女间没有纯洁的友情。

Yet in reality, as gender roles loosen and equality becomes a norm in the workplace, it has become much more common for **platonic** friendships to blossom.

但在现实生活中，随着性别角色意识淡化，男女平等成为职场的规范，男女之间的柏拉图式友谊也更为普遍地肆意增长了。

"The belief that men and women can't be friends comes from another era in which women were at home and men were in the workplace, and the only way they could get together was for romance," explains psychologist Linda Sapadin to *Psychology Today* magazine. "Now they work together and share sports interests and **socialize** together."

心理学家琳达·萨帕丁在接受《今日心理学》杂志采访时解释道："男女不能成为朋友这种说法产生于另外一个时代，那时女人在家，男人工作，只有通过爱情他们才能待在一起。而如今，男人和女人一起工作、享有共同的体育爱好，一起参加社交活动。"

Today, the main **obstacle** to cross-gender friendships is often **jealousy** from a romantic partner. To overcome this, communication is **essential.**

"My boyfriend has met all of my guy friends so he's quite accepting of me hanging out with them," says Nellie. "Because we've been dating so long, there's a level of trust where he knows I will make the right decision when choosing who to be friends with."

"He understands that the kind of time that I spend differs between guys and girls. When I'm out with the girls, we're gossiping or talking about clothes but when I'm spending time with the guys, it's different. I think their carefree and 'whatever goes' attitude can sometimes be exactly what I need."

现如今，这种跨越性别的友谊所面临的主要障碍往往是另一半的嫉妒，想要克服这点，沟通交流尤为重要。

"我的男友见过我所有的男闺蜜，所以对于我与他们一起打发时间这件事，他毫无怨言。"奈丽说，"我俩已经约会很长时间了，对彼此的信任已经到达了一定高度，他知道我能够在交友方面做出自己正确的选择。"

"他懂得我与男生和女生在一起时玩的不同之处。如果我和女伴们出去，我会聊聊八卦和衣服，但如果是和男生一起情况就不一样了，有时候他们那无所谓、放任自流的态度正是我所需要的。"

单词解析 Word Analysis

potential [pə'tenʃl] *adj.* 潜在的，有可能的

例 The firm has identified 60 potential customers at home and abroad.

该公司已在国内外找到60个潜在客户。

alternative [ɔːl'tɜːnətɪv] *adj.* 可供选择的，可替代的

例 New ways to treat arthritis may provide an alternative to painkillers.

关节炎的新疗法可能是代替止痛药的另一种选择。

somewhat ['sʌmwɒt] *adv.* 有点儿，有几分

例 He explained somewhat unconvincingly that company was paying for everything.

他解释说公司会支付一切费用，这个说法有点儿令人不能信服。

judgmental [dʒʌdʒ'mentl] *adj.* 主观判断的，武断的

例 I think that he is too judgmental to be a good therapist.

我认为他太主观，不会成为一个好的临床医学家。

pressure ['preʃə(r)] *n.* 压力

例 The pressure of his fingers had relaxed.

他手指按压的力道减轻了。

platonic [plə'tɒnɪk] *adj.* 柏拉图式的

例 She values the platonic friendship she has had with Chris for ten years.

她珍惜自己和克里斯之间长达10年的柏拉图式的友情。

socialize ['səʊʃəlaɪz] *v.* 进行社交活动，与人交往

例 It distressed her that she and Charles no longer socialized with old friends.

她和查尔斯不再跟老朋友们来往，这让她非常苦恼。

obstacle ['ɒbstəkl] *n.* 障碍物

例 Most competition cars will only roll over if they hit an obstacle.

大多数赛车只有在撞上障碍物时才会翻车。

jealousy ['dʒeləsi] *n.* 嫉妒

例 At first his jealousy only showed in small ways.

起初他的小心眼表现得不是十分明显。

essential [ɪ'senʃl] *adj.* 必不可少的，基本的

例 As they must also sprint over short distances, speed is essential.

由于他们也必须进行短跑，因此速度至关重要。

语法知识点 Grammar Points

① When dealing with male relatives, coworkers and even boyfriends, another man's point of view can be incredibly useful.

point of view 观点

例 I have some sympathy with this point of view.
我在一定程度上赞同这个观点。

例 From the point of view of fire, those shanties are complete death traps.
从防火角度看，那些简陋小木屋绝对是死亡陷阱。

② Most relationships between males and females that we come across in our day-to-day lives...

come across 偶遇

例 I've never come across hieroglyphics like the handwriting of Peter Smallwood.
我从未见过像彼得·斯莫尔伍德那样潦草难辨的笔迹。

③ My boyfriend has met all of my guy friends so he's quite accepting of me hanging out with them.

hang out with sb. 经常与某人泡在一起

例 I used to hang out with a pretty wild crowd.
我过去常常跟一群放荡不羁的人闲逛。

经典名句 *Famous Classics*

1. Genius only means hard-working all one's life.
天才只意味着终身不懈地努力。

2. Live a noble and honest life. Reviving past times in your old age will help you to enjoy your life again.
过一种高尚而诚实的生活。当你年老时回想起过去，你就能再一次享受人生。

3. One's courtesy is a mirror to see his image.

一个人的礼貌是一面照出他肖像的镜子。

4. If you are not in good control of time or cannot set priorities for different matters, what you do is surely to be rebated.
不能充分掌握时间与区别事情的缓急先后，你的一切都会打折扣。

5. Every flatterer lives at the expense of those who listen to him.
阿谀奉承的人正是靠听信谗言的人活命的。

6. Life is to talk after a respite and not to act ahead of schedule.
生命就是且缓一口气再讲，明天再说明天的。

7. All the splendor in the world is not worth a good friend.
人世间所有的荣华富贵不如一个好朋友。

8. Honesty and diligence should be your eternal mates.
诚实与勤勉应该成为你永久的伴侣。

读书笔记

15 American Friendship
美式友谊

Steve and Yaser first met in their **chemistry** class at an American university. Yaser was an international student from Jordan. He was excited to get to know an American. He wanted to learn more about American culture. Yaser hoped that he and Steve would become good friends.

史帝夫和亚瑟最初是在一所美国大学的化学课上认识的。亚瑟是从约旦来的国际学生。他很兴奋能够认识美国人，他要学习更多美国文化；亚瑟希望他和史帝夫会成为好朋友。

At first, Steve seemed very **friendly**. He always greeted Yaser **warmly** before class. Sometimes he offered to study with Yaser. He even invited Yaser to eat lunch with him. But after the **semester** was over, Steve seemed more **distant**. The two former classmates didn't see each other very much at school. One day Yaser decided to call Steve. Steve didn't seem very interested in talking to him. Yaser was hurt by Steve's change of **attitude**. "Steve said we were friends," Yaser complained. "And I thought friends were friends forever."

刚开始史帝夫似乎非常友善，上课前他总是热情地和亚瑟打招呼，有时他和亚瑟一起读书；他甚至邀请亚瑟一起共进午餐。但是学期结束后，史帝夫似乎较冷淡了，这两个以前是同学的人在学校不常碰面了。有一天，亚瑟决定打电话给史帝夫，史帝夫似乎没有兴趣和他讲话。对于史帝夫态度的改变，亚瑟感到受伤害。“史帝夫曾说我们是朋友，”亚瑟抱怨，“而且我认为一朝是朋友就永远是朋友。”

Yaser is a little **confused**. He is an outsider to American culture. He doesn't understand the way Americans view friendship. Americans use the word friend in a very general way. They may call both **casual** acquaintances and

亚瑟有点儿困惑了，对于美国文化，他是个局外人（外行）。他不了解美国人对友谊的看法。美国人把“朋友”这个字用得非常广泛，一般的泛泛之交和亲密伙伴都算是朋

close **companions** "friends." Americans have school friends, work friends, sports friends and neighborhood friends. These friendships are based on common interests. When the shared activity ends, the friendship may fade. Now Steve and Yaser are no longer classmates. Their friendship has changed.

In some cultures friendship means a strong life-long bond between two people. In these cultures friendships develop slowly, since they are built to last. American society is one of **rapid** change. Studies show that one out of five American families moves every year. American friendships develop quickly, and they may change just as quickly.

友。美国人的朋友包含有学校的朋友、工作的朋友、运动的朋友或是街坊邻居。这些友谊都是建立在共同的兴趣上，当共同从事的活动结束时，友谊也可能随之消失了。现在，史帝夫和亚瑟不再是同学，他们的友谊也就改变了。

在一些文化里，友谊即两人之间一种强烈的、一世之久的情感。在这些文化里，友谊发展得慢，因为要持久。但美国是个急速变迁的社会，有些研究发现每年每五个美国家庭之中，就有一个家庭搬家。美国人的友谊建立得快，但也可能改变得快。

单词解析 *Word Analysis*

chemistry ['kemɪstri] *n.* 化学

例 We have literally altered the chemistry of our planet's atmosphere.
我们确实改变了地球大气层的化学构成。

friendly ['frendli] *adj.* 友好的，友善的

例 Godfrey had been friendly to me.
戈弗雷一度对我很友善。

warmly [wɔːmlɪ] *adv.* 温暖地，热情地

例 He warmly shook hands with those gathered around the rostrum.
他同聚集在主席台四周的人热情握手。

semester [sɪ'mestə(r)] *n.* 学期

例 A student will probably attend four or five courses during each semester.

每个学生一学期可能要修四五门课程。

distant ['dɪstənt] *adj.* 遥远的，远距离的

例 The mountains rolled away to a distant horizon.

群山向远处的地平线绵延而去。

attitude ['ætɪtjuːd] *n.* 态度，看法

例 Being unemployed produces negative attitudes to work.

失业会产生对工作的消极态度。

confused [kən'fjuːzd] *adj.* 迷惑的

例 A survey showed people were confused about what they should eat to stay healthy.

一项调查表明，人们对该吃什么才能保持健康这个问题感到困惑。

casual ['kæʒuəl] *adj.* 漫不经心的，随意的

例 It's difficult for me to be casual about anything.

要我轻松处事很难。

companion [kəm'pæniən] *n.* 同伴，伙伴

例 Fred had been her constant companion for the last six years of her life.

在她生命的最后6年，弗莱德一直是她忠实的伴侣。

rapid ['ræpɪd] *adj.* 快速的，迅速的

例 This signals a rapid change of mind by the government.

这标志着政府思想的急剧转变。

语法知识点 *Grammar Points*

① These friendships are based on common interests.

base on 把……建立在；以……为基础

例 One should always base one's opinion on facts.
人们说话应以事实为根据。

base用作动词是“把……建立在，以……为基础”的意思，指人们依据一定的客观规律或自己的亲身体验而得出的一定结论。base常用于非物质结构的基础，这个基础可以是物质的，也可以是非物质的。

② Now Steve and Yaser are no longer classmates. Their friendship has changed.

no longer 表示时间或距离的“不再”延长，意为“如今不再”，等于not... any longer

例 When there is no gravity, our feet no longer stay on the ground.
如果没有重力，我们的脚就不能再站稳在地面上。

no longer / not...any longer表示不再继续或再现过去某一时刻发生或存在而一直延续的动作/状态时，常用于过去时、现在时或将来时的句子中。如：

例 He was no longer a thief.
他不再是小偷了。

当修饰动词时，no longer 通常位于句中的实意动词之前，动词be、助动词和情态动词之后，有时也可位于句末或句首(用于句首时，其后用倒装语序)，可用于延续性动词和非延续性动词，此时也可用 not...any more 或not...any longer。

例 She could no longer find a way to get into the valley.
她再也找不到进山谷的路了。

例 Time or opportunity lost will return no more.
机不可失，时不再来。

③ Studies show that one out of five American families moves every year.

one out of five 表示比率，如果用作主语，从理论上说，谓语应用单数，因为句子的实际主语是one，但实际上也可以用复数。

例 One man in five was unemployed.
每五人中有一人失业。

例 About one in every 20 people have clinical depression.
大约每20个人中有1个患有临床抑郁症。

经典名句 *Famous Classics*

1. Take a deep breath. If you're mad, give yourself time to calm down. You want to be sure you really want to end the friendship.
深吸一口气。如果你快气疯了，给自己时间冷静下来。你要确定自己真的想要结束两人之间的友谊。

2. Try a temporary separation. You might find you miss each other and want to get back together. Hey, it has worked for married couples.
尝试暂时分开，你可能发现你们都想念对方，希望恢复交往。至少这种方法对夫妻是有效的。

3. Go slowly, especially if it's a close relationship.
慢慢来，特别是如果你们是非常要好的朋友。

4. The time to be up-front and honest with your friends is before a breakup.
真要到了分手的时候，你再对朋友直截了当地说实话。

读书笔记

16 How to Finish off a Friendship? 如何结束友谊

Dissolving a friendship is harder than ever these days, with so many digital ties holding us together, from social-networking Web sites like Facebook to stored numbers in cellphones.

与朋友分手如今变得比以往更难了，因为有那么多的数字纽带将我们连在一起，从Facebook等社交网站到手机上存储的电话号码。

Dave Nadkarni can tell you all about it. When he decided to end a relationship a few years ago with a close **female** friend he felt she was spreading rumors about him, he stopped returning her calls, **defriended** her on Facebook, **blocked** her on his instant-message list, stopped following her on Twitter and changed her name in his cellphone to "Do Not Pick Up." "It was **cathartic**," he says.

大卫·纳德卡尼对此深有感触。几年前他决定和一位他觉得说自己坏话的红颜知己绝交的时候，他不回她的电话，在Facebook不再把她列为好友，在即时消息名单上把她屏蔽掉，不再关注她的"推文"，把手机中她的名字改成了"不要接听"。他说，这真像是来了一场大扫除。

But it didn't work. His friend got the hint and stopped calling him, and he has successfully avoided seeing her in real life. But he still runs into her constantly online, every time a mutual friend retweets her Twitter posts or she leaves a comment on a mutual Facebook friend's status update.

不过却没有用。他的那个女性朋友明白了他的暗示，不再给他打电话，现实生活中他也成功地得以避免再见到她。不过他仍会经常在网上碰到她，比如每次他们共同的朋友把她的"推文"转给他，或是她在共同的Facebook朋友的状态更新中留言的时候。

"It sucks," says Mr. Nadkarni, 29, a sales rep for a security company in Las Vegas. "It's like the dog that's stuck on your leg that you can't shake off."

现年29岁的纳德卡尼是拉斯维加斯一家安保公司的销售代表。他说，太糟糕了，就像是一只咬着你腿不放、你怎么

So how do you finish off a friendship? Are some ways better than others? Psychologists recommend ending a friendship in a way that avoids **collateral** damage with mutual friends, spouses and coworkers, and allows you to start it up again later, if you want. So don't hurl insults. Don't assign blame. Try to be polite.

That's what happened to Nelson De Sousa. Last spring, he repeatedly got into heated arguments with his two best friends from high school, whom he been close to for more than 20 years. He felt they were too **sympathetic** to his wife's point of view after his divorce. In one day, he screamed at them both on the phone. Each of them hung up on him.

For months after that, Mr. De Sousa says there was a "cold war atmosphere" in the friendship. When he called his friends, they often refused to pick up the phone. When they did, they were **icy** to him.

Finally, he'd had enough. So he left a message for each one of them on their home phones: "Tag, you're it. I'm not playing this game anymore. The ball is in your court." That was last August. He hasn't heard from them since.

Now Mr. De Sousa can't hear any music by bands that were big when

都摆脱不掉的狗。

你是如何结束一场友谊的？有没有什么好的分手方法？

心理学家建议，结束友谊的方式要尽量避免给共同的朋友、配偶和同事造成连带伤害，还要为你以后一旦想要恢复交往留下余地。所以，不要大声谩骂，不要怪罪对方，而是要尽量保持礼貌。

尼尔森·德索萨就有这样的遭遇。去年春天，他和高中时两个最要好的朋友时常陷入激烈的争吵——他们已经是20多年的朋友了。他感觉在自己离婚之后，他们过于同情他妻子的观点。终于有一天，他在电话中冲着两人都大叫了。两个人都挂了他的电话。

德索萨说，之后好几个月，他们的友谊都处于冷战气氛。当他打电话给他们的时候，对方常常拒绝接听。即使是接了，对他的态度也是冷冰冰的。

最后，他受够了。所以，他分别在两人家里的电话上留言说，好吧，我不再玩这个游戏了，球现在在你那半场了。这件事是去年8月份发生的，之后他再也没有收到他们的消息。

现在，德索萨每每听到高中时热门乐队演奏的音乐，比

he was in high school, such as Duran Duran, New Order, R.E.M. or James, without feeling sad. And to make matters worse, he got engaged last week and would love to share the news with his old friends.

"I was the cutter-offer," says Mr. De Sousa, 37, a trade compliance manager from Union, N.J. "But perhaps it wasn't the best **strategy**."

如杜兰杜兰(Duran Duran)、New Order、R.E.M.或是James，就会感到伤心。更糟糕的是，上周他订婚了，他真想和自己的老朋友分享这个好消息。

德索萨现年37岁，是新泽西州的一名贸易合规经理。他说，是我和他们一刀两断了，但或许这并不是最好的策略。

单词解析 *Word Analysis*

dissolve [dɪ'zɒlv] *v.* 分裂，溶解，解除

例 They found a number of simple expediencies to dissolve the contract.

他们找出了许多解除合同的简便方法。

female ['fiːmeɪl] *n.* 女性，女子

例 But the average young female in this country now is stylish and remarkably confident.

但该国普通年轻女子现在都非常时髦，而且极其自信。

defriend [diː'frɛnd] *v.* 拉黑

例 If there's a part of your body we don't like, we'll just defriend it.

要是我们不喜欢你身体上什么部分，也就取消关注罢了。

block [blɒk] *v.* 限制，阻塞，堵塞

例 Some students today blocked a highway that cuts through the center of the city.

今天一些学生堵塞了一条贯穿市中心的公路。

cathartic [kə'θɑːtɪk] *adj.* 宣泄情绪的

例 His laughter was cathartic, an animal yelp that brought tears to his eyes.
他哈哈大笑以宣泄情绪，声音如野兽般尖厉，眼泪都笑出来了。

collateral [kə'lætərəl] *n.* 担保物，抵押物

例 Many people use personal assets as collateral for small business loans.
很多人把个人财产用作小额商业贷款的抵押品。

sympathetic [ˌsɪmpə'θetɪk] *adj.* 同情的；赞同的；讨人喜欢的

例 It may be that he sees you only as a sympathetic friend.
也许他只是把你当作一个可以倾诉的朋友。

icy ['aɪsi] *adj.* 冰冷的，极冷的

例 His shoes and clothes were wet through and icy cold.
他的鞋和衣服都湿透了，冰冷冰冷的。

strategy ['strætədʒi] *n.* 策略

例 What should our marketing strategy have achieved?
我们的销售策略应该取得了哪些成果呢？

语法知识点 *Grammar Points*

① But he still runs into her constantly online, every time a mutual friend retweets her Twitter posts or she leaves a comment on a mutual Facebook friend's status update.

run into 有着几个不同的含义，并且可以被用于不同的语境当中

表示偶然遇到某人

例 We live in the same neighbourhood but we never run into each other.
我们住在同一个街区，但是我们从来没有碰到过对方。

表示碰撞到某物

例 There is a very low chance you will run into that boat. Don't worry!

你撞到那艘船的概率很小。不用担心！

表示经历困境或遇见问题

例 We ran into issues within the first few months of the project.
我们在这项工程的前几个月就遇到了一些问题。

② In one day, he screamed at them both on the phone. Each of them hung up on him.

on the phone 在打电话

例 They should talk about it on the phone.
他们可以在电话中谈论它。

例 I explained what happened and he gave me a ticket for talking on the phone while driving.
在我解释了一通之后，他因为我在开车的时候打电话而给了我一张罚单。

hung up on 挂断某人的电话

例 Why did you hang up on me? It's rude.
你怎么把我的电话给挂了？太不像话了。

③ And to make matters worse, he got engaged last week and would love to share the news with his old friends.

to make matters worse 是习语，意思是"使情况更糟的是"（主要用作插入语）

例 To make matters worse, my friend then lost her keys.
更为糟糕的是，我的朋友又弄丢了她的钥匙。

除用作插入语外，也可用于谓语部分

例 Let him say what he will; he cannot make matters worse.
不管他说什么，他也不会使事态变得更糟了。

经典名句 *Famous Classics*

1. Issue an ultimatum—but be prepared to lose your friends.
发最后通牒，不过你要准备好失去你的朋友。

2. A friend in court is better than a penny in purse.
囊中有钱，不如朝中有友。

3. If I should meet thee, after long years, how should I greet thee with silence and tears.
多年离别后，抑或再相逢，相逢何所语，泪流默无声！

4. You are the best friend because you always can listen to what I don't say!
你是那位可以听到我内心深处的朋友！

5. If you wish to succeed, you should use persistence as your good friend, experience as your reference, prudence as your brother and hope as your sentry.
如果你希望成功，当以恒心为良友，以经验为参谋，以谨慎为兄弟，以希望为哨兵。

读书笔记

17 Some Friendships End Badly 有些友谊则是不欢而散

Others end badly. Rob Wilson, 53, a writer in Atlanta, saw a 12-year friendship **abruptly** end after he mentioned he was voting for George W. Bush in the 2004 presidential election. Arthur Newton, 46, a hotel manager from Austin, Texas, had a female friend who tell him she couldn't hang out with him anymore because her husband was jealous.

有些则是不欢而散。53岁的罗伯·威尔逊是亚特兰大的一位作家。在2004年的总统大选中，他向朋友提到自己投了布什的票，之后两人之间12年的友谊就戛然而止了。得克萨斯州奥斯汀46岁的酒店经理亚瑟·牛顿的一个女性朋友告诉他，因为她丈夫嫉妒，所以她无法继续和他做朋友了。

Michael Hassard watched a good friend run away from him—literally. He had heard his pal had begun dating his ex-girlfriend, so Mr. Hassard, 39, a NASA engineer from Muscle Shoals, Ala., **approached** him in church one day to ask about it. But before he could speak, his friend turned and fled down a **hallway,** out the door and into his car. He and his former buddy never spoke again.

迈克尔·哈萨德眼睁睁地看着他的一个好朋友从他身边跑掉了。哈萨德39岁，是驻阿拉巴马州的一名美国国家航空及太空总署（NASA）工程师。他听说朋友开始与自己的前女友约会，所以有一天他在教堂见到他时，想上前问个究竟。可是还没等他开口，朋友就转身沿着走廊跑掉了，跑到门外之后进了自己的车。两人从此再没说过话。

Friendships are such a **nuanced** and **intriguing** relationship that we even follow celebrity friend breakups, as we do their romances. Why else would we care about Mariana Pasternak but for her tell-all book about her former friendship

友谊是一种微妙而动人的关系，我们甚至会像关注名人情侣分手一样关注名人朋友分手。如果不是玛丽安娜·巴斯特纳克那本有关她和“家政女皇”玛莎·斯图尔特从前友谊的“全

with Martha Stewart, which ended after Ms. Pasternak testified at Ms. Stewart's 2004 trial.

"It's a myth that friendships last forever." says Irene S. Levine, a psychologist, professor of **psychiatry** at New York University's medical school and author of *Best Friends Forever: Surviving a Breakup with Your Best Friend*. "We are tied to our family by blood and our spouses by law, so we are often more attentive to those relationships. Friendships are relationships of choice, so we tend to overlook them." she says.

As a result, many friendships die from neglect, Dr. Levine says. And this in itself poses a very sticky problem in friendship breakups: How do you know if you're being **neglected**—or dumped? What if your friend is always too busy to get together but always seems to have a good excuse? What if she never calls you, but seems happy enough to hear from you when you call?

And there's the rub. There are no rules or even societal norms for friendship **breakups**. Friends who want to split don't go to counseling or get a mediator or a lawyer, as divorcing couples do. And there typically aren't a bunch of nosy relatives willing to

揭秘"书，我们又怎么会关注她呢？2004年斯图尔特受审时，巴斯特纳克曾出庭作证，之后两人的友谊就结束了。

纽约大学医学院精神病学教授、心理学家艾琳·莱文说，友谊地久天长的说法纯粹是天方夜谭。她曾著有《永远都是好朋友》一书。她说，我们与家人之间靠血缘关系维系，和配偶之间靠法律关系维系，所以我们对家人和配偶更用心；友谊则是你选择的，所以我们往往会忽视。

莱文说，结果就造成很多友谊因为忽视而告终。这本身就给朋友之间的分手带来了一个非常棘手的问题：你如何知道自己被忽视了，或被"抛弃"了？如果你的朋友总是看起来忙得无法和你见面，又总是看起来有很好的理由怎么办？如果她从来不给你打电话，但在你打给她的时候看起来很高兴呢？

问题是，对于朋友之间的分手，并没有什么规则可言，甚至没有社交惯例可循。要分手的朋友不会像离婚的夫妻一样去找顾问咨询，或是找个调解人或律师。与夫妻分手不同的是，朋友分手通常也没有一

intervene and relay messages, as there are when a split is within a family.

大群叽叽喳喳的亲戚想要干预或在中间传话。

单词解析 *Word Analysis*

abruptly [ə'brʌptlɪ] *adv.* 突然地，意外地

例 Then abruptly he revved the engine to full power.
然后他突然加速到最大马力。

approach [ə'prəʊtʃ] *v.* 接近

例 He didn't approach the front door at once.
他没有马上走向前门。

hallway ['hɔːlweɪ] *n.* 走廊

例 She climbed the steps and proceeded along the upstairs hallway.
她爬上楼梯，顺着楼上的走廊走去。

nuanced ['njuːɑːnst] *adj.* 有细微差别的

例 The World Health Organization has given a more nuanced response.
世界卫生组织（WHO）提供了更为微妙的回应。

intriguing [ɪn'triːgɪŋ] *adj.* 有趣的，迷人的

例 This intriguing book is both thoughtful and informative.
这本引人入胜的书既有思想性又富知识性。

psychiatry [saɪ'kaɪətri] *n.* 精神病学，精神病疗法

例 Psychiatry has the character of interdisciplinary.
精神病学具有跨学科性质。

neglect [nɪ'glekt] *v.* 疏忽，忽略

例 The woman denied that she had neglected her child.
那位女士否认疏于照管自己的孩子。

breakup ['breɪk'ʌp] *n.* 破裂，终结

例 Since the break-up of his marriage he had not formed any new relationships.
他婚姻破裂后没有谈新朋友。

语法知识点 *Grammar Points*

① Arthur Newton, 46, a hotel manager from Austin, Texas, had a female friend who tell him she couldn't hang out with him anymore because her husband was jealous.

hang out 闲逛，逗留

例 I used to hang out with a pretty wild crowd.
我过去常常跟一群放荡不羁的人闲逛。

例 We are fools to hang out at noon. It's dying hot today.
我们选择中午出来逛街，真是不明智，今天太热了。

还有一个用法，表示"把……晾出去"

例 I was worried I wouldn't be able to hang my washing out.
我担心自己没法把洗好的衣服晾出去。

② Michael Hassard watched a good friend run away from him—literally.

run away 走掉；逃脱；（使）流走

例 He had a terrible urge to run away and hide.
他有一种想要逃离并躲起来的强烈冲动。

例 Most of the victims were shot while trying to run away.
大多数遇害者是在试图逃走的时候中枪的。

③ As a result, many friendships die from neglect

die from 死于（某种原因，不包括疾病、过度悲伤等）

例 Every year, several people die from carbon monoxide poisoning.
每年都有数人死于一氧化碳中毒。

表示死的原因，die后既可接介词of，也可接 from，两者的区别是：
①若死因存在于人体之上或之内（主要指疾病、衰老等自身的原因），一般用介词of。如：die of illness (heart trouble, cancer, a fever, etc) 死于疾病（心脏病、癌症、发烧等）
②若死因不是存在人体之内或之上，而是由环境造成的（主要指事故等方面的外部原因），一般用介词from。如：die from an earthquake (a traffic accident, a lightning, a stroke, etc) 死于地震（交通事故、雷击等）
③若死因是环境影响到体内，即两方面共有的原因，则of和from均可。如：die of [from] a drink (a wound, overwork, starvation, hunger and cold, etc) 死于饮酒（受伤、劳累过度、饥饿、饥寒等）但是在实际运用中，两者混用的情况较多。

经典名句 *Famous Classics*

1. Everything is good when new, but friend when old.
东西新的好，朋友老的好。

2. A thousand friends are few; one enemy is too many.
朋友千人尚觉少，仇敌一人犹嫌多。

3. When a friend asks, there is no tomorrow.
朋友的要求不要拖。

4. Choose an author as you choose a friend.
选书如择友。

5. A true friend is one soul in two bodies.
真正的朋友好似两个身子长着一颗心。

6. A joke never gains an enemy but often loses a friend.
开玩笑总不能化敌为友，反而有时会失去朋友。

7. A near friend is better than a far-dwelling kinsman.
远亲不如近邻。

8. A man without friends is an angel without wings, whose life will suffer in the long tolerance of loneliness and depression.
一个人没有朋友，就如一个天使没有羽翼，长期生活在寂寞与沮丧的折磨之下。

18 Many Friendships Just Don't Last 很多友谊就是无法维持很久

Linda Lajterman suffered one of the worst experiences of her life while on a **cruise** with her husband and two other couples. Halfway through the trip, one of her friends stopped talking to her—for good.

琳达·拉哲特曼在与丈夫和另外两对夫妇乘船游览的时候遭遇了她这辈子最不愉快的经历。半路上，她的一个朋友不理她了，而且永远不理她了。

Ms. Lajterman says she has no idea what **prompted** the woman, who was one of her best friends, to cut her off. They helped take care of each other's kids, celebrated family events together and shared **confidences**. After the cruise, which took place a few years ago, she called her friend and asked for an explanation, but received none. She says she was **devastated**.

拉哲特曼说，她不知道是什么事让最好的朋友和她绝交了。她们曾帮对方照看小孩，一起举办家庭庆祝活动，分享秘密。在旅行过后，她打电话给那个朋友，请她做出解释，不过对方什么也没说，这已经是几年前的事了。拉哲特曼说，她因此感到很伤心。

"I would have welcomed the opportunity to **apologize** or discuss it if I did anything wrong," says Ms. Lajterman, a 52-year-old nurse from Ramsey, N.J. "Instead, it took me three self-help books and two years to make peace with the fact that someone I thought was a good friend ended our friendship."

现年52岁的拉哲特曼是新泽西州拉姆齐的一名护士。她说，如果是我做错了什么事，我希望有机会道歉，或者和她好好谈谈。相反，我却是在读了三本自助书，花了两年的时间后才让自己接受了这个事实——我以为是好朋友的人和我绝交了。

There are 50 ways to leave your lover, according to Paul Simon. But how many ways are there to leave a friend?

正如保罗·西蒙在歌中唱到的，离开情人的方法有50种。不过，离开朋友的方法有多少种呢？

I know, it's a terrible question. But think about it: Some of the worst breakups in our lives are not with **romantic** partners. They are with friends—the people with whom we often share our deepest thoughts. Friends provide guidance, encouragement, laughter and a refuge. Losing a good friend can be one of the saddest experiences in life.

我知道，这个问题很可怕。不过好好想想：我们人生中最糟糕的分手经历有些并不是和情人之间。有些是和朋友——那些我们经常分享自己内心深处想法的人。朋友能够给你指引、鼓励、欢笑和避风港。失去一个好朋友有可能是一辈子最让人难过的经历之一。

And yet, many friendships just don't last. Some simply fizzle out, victims of routine life events such as moves, job changes, divorce or a **divergence** of interests.

不过，很多友谊就是无法持久。有些是无疾而终，成为搬家、工作变动、离婚和兴趣不同等普通人生过程的牺牲品。

单词解析 *Word Analysis*

cruise [kruːz] *n.* 乘船游览，航游

例 He and his wife were planning to go on a world cruise.
他和太太计划乘船环游世界。

prompt [prɒmpt] *v.* 促使，导致

例 Japan's recession has prompted consumers to cut back on buying cars.
日本经济的不景气使得消费者在购买车辆上减少了开支。

confidence ['kɒnfɪdəns] *n.* 秘密

例 We told you all these things in confidence.
我们告诉你的这些事都需要保密。

devastated ['devəsteɪtɪd] *adj.* 极为震惊的

例 Bishop Daly said he was devastated by news of the Cardinal's death.
戴利主教说他听到红衣主教去世的消息后感到极为震惊和难过。

apologize [ə'pɒlədʒaɪz] *v.* 道歉

例 Two years ago, Congress formally apologized for the internment.
两年前，国会就此拘留事件正式道歉。

romantic [rəʊ'mæntɪk] *adj.* 浪漫的

例 They enjoyed a romantic dinner for two at one of their favourite restaurants.
他俩在他们最喜欢的一家餐馆里吃了一顿浪漫的二人晚餐。

refuge ['refjuːdʒ] *n.* 避难所，安全地带

例 We climbed up a winding track towards a mountain refuge.
我们沿着一条蜿蜒的小道爬向山上的一处避难所。

divergence [daɪ'vɜːdʒəns] *n.* 分歧，差异

例 There's a substantial divergence of opinion within the party.
党内存在着重大的意见分歧。

语法知识点 *Grammar Points*

① Halfway through the trip, one of her friends stopped talking to her—for good.

stop doing sth. 停止做某事（停止正在做的事情）

例 He stopped watching TV and began to read English.
他停下来看电视，开始读英语。

stop to do sth. 意为"停下来原来做的事，做下面的事"

例 He watched TV for an hour; at 8 he stopped to do his homework.
他看了一个小时的电视，八点钟他停下来（看电视）去做作业。

for good 永远

例 She says that she is leaving the country for good.
她说她要永远离开这个国家。

例 She had hoped to get rid of the girl for good and all.
她原想一劳永逸地把这个姑娘赶走。

② After the cruise, which took place a few years ago, she called her friend and asked for an explanation, but received none.

固定词组take place意为发生，举行，多指举行活动，发生某事（可指发生好事或不好的事），一般指非偶然性事件的“发生”，即这种事件的发生一定有某种原因或事先的安排。

例 Great changes have taken place in China.
中国发生了翻天覆地的变化。

例 The meeting will take place next Friday.
会议将在下周五举行。

英语中表示“发生”常用的是happen，用于表示偶然发生的、没有预料到的事情。

例 The accident happened on the Sunday night.
事故发生在星期日晚上。

happen to do 意思是：碰巧。

例 It happened to be a fine one that day.
那天碰巧天气好。

It happens that... 后接从句，意思也是碰巧。

例 It happens that his sister is a closed friend of mine.
碰巧她姐姐是我的一个好朋友。

例 It so happened that both of them were there.
正好他们两个人都在那儿。

③ Instead, it took me three self-help books and two years to make peace with the fact that someone I thought was a good friend ended our friendship.

It take sb. sth. to do 花费某人……做什么，it是形式主语；其真正主语是动词不定式“to do sth.”。

例 It took me half an hour to do my homework.
我花了半个小时做作业。

④ Losing a good friend can be one of the saddest experiences in life.

losing a good friend是动名词短语做主语的用法。

例 Forgetting the past means betrayal.
忘记过去就意味着背叛。

例 Asking for advice on the Internet is not helpful for your study.
在网络上寻求建议对你的学习是没有帮助的。

经典名句 *Famous Classics*

1. Friends are like fiddle-strings; they must not be screwed too tight.
朋友像琴弦，不能拧太紧。

2. Without a friend the world is a wilderness.
没有朋友，世界就等于一片荒野。

3. Between friends all is common.
朋友之间不分彼此。

4. In time of prosperity, friends will be plenty; in time of adversity, not one amongst twenty.
富在深山有远亲，穷在闹市无人理。

5. A father is a treasure, a brother is a comfort, but a friend is both.
父亲是财富，兄弟是安慰，朋友兼而有之。

6. Trust not the praise of a friend, nor the contempt of an enemy.
不要信赖朋友的赞扬，也不要把仇敌的轻蔑放在心上。

7. Friendship the older it grows the stronger it is.
友谊地久天长。

8. Familiar paths and old friends are the best.
熟路好遵循，老友最可珍。

19 Friends (I) 朋友（I）

On my recent travels, I came to realize still more fully the significance of the word "friend". Seven or eight days ago, I said to a friend whom I had just come to know, "I can't help feeling embarrassed before my friends. You're all so nice to me. I simply don't know how to repay your **kindness**." I did not make this remark out of mere modesty and courtesy. I truly meant what I said. The next day, I said goodbye to this friend, not knowing if I could ever see him again. But the little warmth that he gave me has been keeping my heart throbbing with **gratitude**.

最近一次的旅行使我更了解一个名词的意义，这个名词就是：朋友。七八天以前我曾对一个初次见面的朋友说："在朋友们面前我只感到惭愧。你们待我太好了，我简直没法报答你们。"这并不是谦虚的客气话，这是真的事实。说过这些话，我第二天就离开了那个朋友，并不知道以后还有没有机会再看见他。但是他给我的那一点点温暖至今还使我的心颤动。

The length of my days will not be **unlimited**. However, whenever I look back on my brief past life, I find a beacon illuminating my soul and thereby lending a little brightness to my being. That beacon is friendship. I should be grateful to it because it has helped me keep alive up to now and clear away the shadow left on me by my old family. Many people **forsake** their friends in favor of their own families, or at least draw a line of **demarcation** between families and friends, considering the

我的生命大概不会很长久罢。然而在短促的过去回顾中却有一盏明灯，照彻了我灵魂的黑暗，使我的生存有一点光彩。这盏灯就是友情。我应该感谢它，因为靠了它我才能够活到现在；而且把旧家庭给我留下的阴影扫除了的也正是它。世间有不少的人为了家庭抛弃朋友，至少也会在家庭和朋友之间划一个界限，把家庭看得比朋友重过若干倍。这似乎是很自然的事情。我也曾亲

former to be many times more important than the latter. That seems to be a matter of course. I have also seen with my own eyes how some people abandon their friends as well as their own careers soon after they get married.

眼看见一些人结婚以后就离开朋友，离开事业。

Friends are **transient** whereas family are lasting—that is the tenet, as I know, guiding the behavior of many people. To me, that is utterly **inconceivable**. Without friends, I would have been reduced to I don't know what a **miserable** creature. Friends are my saviors. They give me things which it is beyond my family to give me. Thanks to their **fraternal** love, assistance and encouragement, I have time and again been saved from falling into an abyss while on its verge. They have been enormously **generous** towards me. There was a time when my life was miserable and gloomy. My friends then gave me in large quantities sympathy, love, joy and tears—things essential for existence. It is due to their bountiful free gifts that I also have my share of warmth and happiness in my life. I accepted their kindnesses quietly without ever saying a word of thanks and without ever doing anything in return. In spite of that, my friends never used the epithet "self-centered" when referred to me. They are only too generous towards me.

朋友是暂时的，家庭是永久的。在很多人的行为里我发现了这个信条。这个信条在我实在是不可理解的。对于我，要是没有朋友，我现在会变成怎样可怜的东西，我自己也不知道。然而朋友们把我救了。他们给了我家庭所不能给的东西。他们的友爱，他们的帮助，他们的鼓励，几次把我从深渊的边缘救回来。他们对我表示了无限的慷慨，我的生活曾经是悲苦的、黑暗的。然而朋友们把多量的同情，多量的爱，多量的欢乐，多量的眼泪分给了我，这些东西都是生存所必需的。这些不要报答的慷慨施舍，使我的生活里也有了温暖，有了幸福。我默默地接受了它们。我并不曾说一句感激的话，我也没有做过一件报答的事情。但是朋友们却不把自私的形容词加到我的身上。对于我，他们太慷慨了。

单词解析 *Word Analysis*

kindness ['kaɪndnəs] n. 仁慈，体贴

例 We have been treated with such kindness by everybody.
每个人对我们都很好。

gratitude ['grætɪtjuːd] n. 感激，感谢

例 I wish to express my gratitude to Kathy Davis for her immense practical help.
凯西·戴维斯实实在在地帮了大忙，我想对她表示感谢。

unlimited [ʌn'lɪmɪtɪd] adj. 无限的，（数量）极大的

例 You'll also have unlimited access to the swimming pool.
进泳池的次数是没有限制的。

forsake [fə'seɪk] v. 将……弃之不顾；遗弃；抛弃

例 I still love him and I would never forsake him.
我仍然爱着他，我永远不会离他而去。

demarcation [ˌdiːmaː'keɪʃn] n. 界限的划定

例 It was hard to draw clear lines of demarcation between work and leisure.
在工作和闲暇之间很难划出明确的界限。

transient ['trænziənt] adj. 短暂的，无常的

例 In most cases, pain is transient.
大多数情况下，疼痛是短暂的。

inconceivable [ˌɪnkən'siːvəbl] adj. 不可想象的，不可思议的

例 It was inconceivable to me that Toby could have been my attacker.
真想不到托比竟会是袭击我的人。

miserable ['mɪzrəbl] adj. 悲惨的，令人痛苦的

例 She went to bed, miserable and depressed.
她伤心而沮丧地上床睡觉。

fraternal [frə'tɜːnl] *adj.* 兄弟的，兄弟般的，友好的

例 He said he hoped the issue could be solved in a fraternal way.
他表示希望这个问题能以友好的方式解决。

generous ['dʒenərəs] *adj.* 慷慨的，大方的

例 German banks are more generous in their lending.
德国银行的借贷条件更为宽松。

语法知识点 *Grammar Points*

① I can't help feeling embarrassed before my friends. You're all so nice to me.

can/could not help doing 禁不住(忍不住)做某事

例 We could not help laughing when he finished the story.
他讲完这个故事后我们忍不住笑起来。

例 I cannot help doing so under these circumstances.
在这样的情况下我不得不这样做。

② I did not make this remark out of mere modesty and courtesy.

out of 出于……的原因

例 They help you out of pity.
他们出于同情而帮助了你。

例 He went only out of curiosity.
他仅仅是由于好奇心才去的。

③ I should be grateful to it because it has helped me keep alive up to now and clear away the shadow left on me by my old family.

up to now 到目前为止，常用于现在完成时

例 Up to now the post of president has been largely ceremonial.
迄今为止总统这一职务主要是礼仪性的。

例 Up to now, I've read as far as the fifth chapter, the second volume of *The War and Peace*.
到今天，我已经读到《战争与和平》的第2卷第5章了。

经典名句 *Famous Classics*

1. A faithful friend is hard to find.
益友难得。

2. Friends may meet, but mountains never greet.
朋友可相逢，高山永分离。

3. To preserve a friend three things are required: to honor him present, praise him absent, and assist him in his necessities.
维持友谊需要三点：当面尊重他，背后赞扬他，需要时帮助他。

4. A bosom friend afar brings distant land near.
海内存知己，天涯若比邻。

5. A Friend is a “gift” of our heart treasures. Thank you for being the treasure in my heart.
朋友是心里的一个宝物，谢谢你成为我心中的珍宝。

6. He is rich enough who has true friends.
有真朋友的人是富翁。

7. Friends must part.
天下无不散之筵席。

读书笔记

20 Friends (II)
朋友（Ⅱ）

I visited many new places and met new friends on my recent trip. My time was mostly taken up by looking around, listening, talking and walking. But I never ran into any trouble because my friends had done their utmost to make sure that I would be short of nothing. Whatever new places I called at, I always felt at home as if I were back in my old **residence** in Shanghai which had been already been raged to the ground by Japanese troops. No matter how hard up and **frugal** my friends themselves were, they would **unstintingly** share with me whatever they had, although they knew I would not be able to repay them for their kindness. Some, whom I did not even know by name, showed concern over my health and went about inquiring after me. It was not until they saw my **suntanned** face and arms that they began to smile a smile of relief. All that was enough to move one to tears.

Some people believe that, without writing, I would lose my livelihood. One of my **sympathizers**, in an article published two months ago in the *Guangzhou Republic Daily Supplement*, gives a full account of the conditions

这一次我走了许多新地方，看见了许多新朋友。我的生活是忙碌的：忙着看，忙着听，忙着说，忙着走。但是我不曾遇到一点儿困难，朋友们给我准备好了一切，使我不会缺少什么。我每走到一个新地方，我就像回到我那个在上海被日本兵毁掉的旧居一样。每一个朋友，不管他自己的生活是怎样苦，怎样简单，也要慷慨地分一些东西给我，虽然明知道我不能够报答他。有些朋友，连他们的名字我以前也不知道，他们却关心我的健康，处处打听我的“病况”，直到他们看见了我那被日光晒黑了的脸和膀子，他们才放心地微笑了，这种情形的确让人感动。

有人相信我不写文章就不能够生活。两个月以前，一个同情我的上海朋友寄稿到《广州民国日报》的副刊，说了许多关于我的生活的话。他也说我一天不写文章第二天就没

of my life. He also says that I would have nothing to live on once I should lay down my pen. That is not true at all. It has already been proved by recent travels that my friends would never let me suffer from cold and hunger even if I should go without writing a single word. There are a great many kind-hearted people in the world who never attach **undue** importance to themselves and their own families and who never place themselves and their families above anything else. It is owing to them that I still survive and shall continue to survive for a long time to come. I owe my friends many, many kindnesses. How can I repay them? But, I understand, they don't need me to do that.

有饭吃。实情不是这样的。这次旅行就给我证明；即使我不再写一个字，朋友们也不肯让我挨饿受冻。世间还有许多慷慨的人，他们并不把自己个人和家庭看得异常重要，超过一切。靠了他们我才能够活到现在，而且靠了他们我还要活下去。朋友们给我的东西太多、太多了。我将怎样报答他们呢？但是我知道他们是不需要报答的。

Recently I came across the following words in a book by a French philosopher: One condition of life is **consumption**... Survival in this world is **inseparable** from generosity, without which we would perish and become dried-up from within. We must put forth flowers. Moral integrity and unselfishness are the flowers of life. Now so many flowers of life are in full bloom before my eyes. When can my life put forth flowers? Am I already dried-up from within?

最近我在一个法国哲学家的书里读到了这样的话："生命的一个条件就是消费……世间有一种不能跟生存分开的慷慨，要是没有了它，我们就会死，就会从内部干枯。我们必须开花。道德和无私心就是人生的花。"在我的眼前开放着这么多的人生的花朵了。我的生命要到什么时候才会开花？难道我已经是"内部干枯"了吗？

A friend of mine says, "If I were a lamp, I would illuminate darkness with

一个朋友说过："我若是灯，我就要用我的光明来照彻

my light." I, however, don't qualify for a bright lamp. Let me be a piece of firewood instead. I'll radiate the heat that I have absorbed from the sun. I'll burn myself to **ashes** to provide this human world with a little warmth.

黑暗。"我不配做一盏明灯。那么就让我做一块木柴罢。我愿意把我从太阳那里受到的热释放出来，我愿意把自己烧得粉身碎骨给人间添一点点温暖。

单词解析 Word Analysis

residence ['rezɪdəns] *n.* 住处，居所

例 She travels constantly, moving among her several residences around the world.

她经常旅行，穿梭于她在世界各地的多处住所。

frugal ['fruːgl] *adj.* 节省的，节约的

例 She lives a frugal life.

她生活俭朴。

unstintingly [ʌn'stɪntɪŋli] *adv.* 慷慨地，大方地

例 I admire it unstintingly, as novel and as human statement.

我无保留地赞赏它，作为小说，也作为人性的陈述。

suntanned ['sʌntænd] *adj.* 晒得黝黑的，晒成古铜色的

例 He is always suntanned and incredibly fit.

他总是皮肤黝黑，无比健康。

sympathizer ['sɪmpəθaɪzə(r)] *n.* 赞同者，支持者

例 These villagers are guerrilla sympathizers.

这些村民拥护游击队。

undue [ˌʌn'djuː] *adj.* 过分的，过多的

例 This would help the families to survive the drought without undue suffering.

这会帮助那些家庭度过干旱期，不至于遭受太多的苦。

consumption [kən'sʌmpʃn] *n.* 消耗量

例 The laws have led to a reduction in fuel consumption in the US.

这些法律已经使美国燃料消费量有所减少。

inseparable [ɪn'seprəbl] *adj.* 不可分割的，分不开的

例 He firmly believes liberty is inseparable from social justice.

他坚信自由与社会正义是不可分的。

ashes ['æʃɪz] *n.* 灰，灰烬

例 A cloud of volcanic ash is spreading across wide areas of the Philippines.

火山灰云层正在菲律宾大范围扩散。

语法知识点 *Grammar Points*

① My time was mostly taken up by looking around, listening, talking and walking.

take up 这个词组有很多意思，上文中译为“占用，花费（时间、空间或精力）”

例 I know how busy you must be and naturally I wouldn't want to take up too much of your time.

我知道您肯定特别忙，我当然不想占用您太多的时间。

除以上意思外，还可译为“占领，占据，占有（位置、阵地）”“喜欢上”“开始从事，开始干（工作）”等。

例 He had taken up a position in the centre of the room.

他占据了房间中心的位置。

例 He did not particularly want to take up a competitive sport.

他并不特别想从事竞技体育运动。

例 He will take up his post as the head of the civil courts at the end of next month.

他将在下个月底就任民事法庭庭长一职。

② But I never ran into any trouble because my friends had done their utmost to make sure that I would be short of nothing.

run into 意为“偶然碰见”

例 I ran into Sally the other day. I could hardly recognize her.
前几天我碰见萨利了，我差点儿没认出她。

表示“遭遇(困难等)”

例 The man knows his daughter has run into trouble.
这个男人知道他的女儿有麻烦了。

表示“驱车造访”

例 The young lady ran into the country with her mother and had a good day.
那个年轻的女士驾车带着她母亲到乡下转了一圈，玩得很开心。

经典名句 *Famous Classics*

1. Better lose a jest than a friend.
宁可不说一句俏皮话，以免得罪朋友们。

2. I've had a great life because I've got you as a real friend.
我的生活因为有了你这个朋友而变得精彩。

3. A true friend is known in the day of adversity.
疾风知劲草，患难见真情。

4. A friend to everybody is a friend to nobody.
广交友，无深交。

5. A friend without faults will never be found.
没有缺点的朋友是永远找不到的。

6. We can live without a brother, but not without a friend.
我们生活中可以没有兄弟，但不能没有朋友。

7. We can live without our friends, but not without our neighbors.
生活可无友，邻居不能无。

8. A friend exaggerates a man's virtue, an enemy his crimes.
朋友宣扬人的美德，敌人夸大人的罪过。

21 How to Make Friends in Challenging Times
如何在逆境中交到朋友

It can be difficult to make friends living in a big city, **especially** when you don't know many people.

生活在一个大城市里是很难交到朋友的，尤其是当你还不认识很多人的时候。

Over years of experience and studying social skills, I discovered that it's possible to make friends without even trying. There are just a few strategies that you have to use on a **consistent** basis.

根据多年的经验以及对社交技能的研究，我发现其实你甚至能毫不费力地交到朋友。这里有一些你一直可以用得上的策略。

That's what I'll **outline** a few simple steps.

在这里我将列出几个简单的步骤。

1. Be seen without trying to get attention.

1. 不刻意地引人注意也能获得他人的注意。

You don't have to say anything witty or interesting to get people's attention; all you have to do is place yourself in environments where people will see you.

你不必说诙谐或有趣的事情来吸引人们的注意，你所要做的只是将你自己置于人们能注意到的地方。

This can be done anywhere you go, such as the supermarket or your yoga **studio**.

这可以在你去的任何地方奏效，比如超市或是瑜伽馆。

2. Use the power of listening.

2. 使用倾听的力量。

There's an interesting **phenomenon** that occurs when you listen to other people, they'll keep talking. Just keep giving them good eye contact and show with your body language that you care.

有一个有趣的现象，当你听别人说话时，他们会一直说话。只要和他们保持良好的眼神接触，并用你的身体语言显示出你对他们的关心。

Listening is a **mechanism** to build trust and likability.

倾听是一种建立信任和魅力的途径。

3. Think about what you can give to the other people.

So often we think about what we can get out of others when we try to make friends, but that thinking needs to be flipped around.

Try offering a piece of helpful advice or invite someone you just met to grab coffee or lunch with you the following week.

4. Always have 3 good stories to tell other people.

When you have at least a few stories to share with others, you'll never run out of things to talk about.

5. Smile like there's no tomorrow.

It may not be natural for some of us to smile, but a smile is one of the most **attractive** things that someone can display when they're meeting new people.

Think about these 5 strategies as tools. They're always available if you want to connect with people **instantly** and develop true lasting friendships.

3. 想想你能给别人什么。

当我们试图交朋友的时候，我们经常会考虑我们能从别人那里得到什么，但是我们需要扭转这种想法。

试着提供一个有用的建议或邀请你刚才遇到的人来喝杯咖啡或者邀请他在接下来的一周和你一起共进午餐。

4. 总是有3个好故事来告诉别人。

当你至少有几个故事与他人分享时，你将永远有谈不尽的话题。

5. 尽情微笑。

对有些人来说，微笑可能是件不自然的事情，但是微笑是最有吸引力的事情之一。当结识新人时，人们可以传递他们的微笑。

我们可以把这5种策略作为工具。如果你想与人立即建立关系，并且发展成真正长久的友谊，它们总是有用的。

单词解析 *Word Analysis*

especially [ɪ'speʃəli] *adv.* 尤其，特别

例 Millions of wild flowers color the valleys, especially in April and May.

尤其是在四五月，不计其数的野花盛开，山谷里一片绚烂色彩。

consistent [kən'sɪstənt] *adj.* 一贯的，一致的，始终如一的

例 Becker has never been the most consistent of players anyway.

不管怎么说，贝克尔从来就不是表现最为稳定的球员。

outline ['aʊtlaɪn] *v.* 概述，概括

例 The methods outlined in this book are only suggestions.

本书概括的一些方法仅供参考。

studio ['stjuːdiəʊ] *n.* 工作室，画室

例 She was in her studio again, painting onto a large canvas.

她又回到了画室，在一张大帆布上作画。

phenomenon [fə'nɒmɪnən] *n.* 现象

例 This form of civil disobedience isn't a particularly new phenomenon.

这种形式的非暴力反抗并不是特别新的现象。

mechanism ['mekənɪzəm] *n.* 方法，途径

例 There's no mechanism for punishing arms exporters who break the rules.

对违规的武器出口商实施惩罚尚无执行机制。

attractive [ə'træktɪv] *adj.* 吸引人的，有魅力的

例 Co-operation was more than just an attractive option; it was an obligation.

合作不仅仅是诱人的选择，它也是一种责任。

instantly ['ɪnstəntli] *adv.* 立刻，马上

例 Some styles are so flattering that they instantly become classics.

有些款式特别衬人，很快就成了经典。

语法知识点 *Grammar Points*

① You don't have to say anything witty or interesting to get people's attention...

anything witty or interesting 形容词作后置定语

单个形容词作定语时，一般放在所修饰的名词之前，但在某些情况下需后置：

修饰somebody, someone, something, anybody, anyone, anything, nobody, nothing等复合不定代词时，本句亦是这种情况。

例 There's nothing wrong with the machine.
机器没有毛病。

当表语形容词作定语时必须放在所修饰的名词之后

例 He must be the best violinist alive.
他一定是当代最好的小提琴手了。

形容词短语作定语必须放在所修饰的名词之后，这时该短语相当于一个定语从句

例 We need a place twice larger than this one.
我们需要一个比这里大一倍的地方。

② When you have at least a few stories to share with others, you'll never run out of things to talk about.

run out of 用完，耗尽（主语只能是人）

例 If we run out of money, we can sell some of the products in Guangzhou.
如果我们的钱用完了，可以在广州卖掉一些产品。

run out和run out of 这两个短语都有“用完”的意思，但用法不同。run out作不及物短语，表示“被用完；被耗尽；（人）把东西用完（或花光）”，其主语通常是时间、金钱、食物等无生命名词，而run out of则是及物短语，表示主动。

例 His strength ran out.
他的力气用完了。

经典名句 *Famous Classics*

1. A ready way to lose a friend is to lend him money.
失友皆从借钱起。

2. Friendship is love with understanding.
友谊是爱加上谅解。

3. Better an open enemy than a false friend.
明枪易躲，暗箭难防。

4. When we meet difficulty, we can lean on each other.
遇困难时，让我们互相扶持!

5. We are good friend forever.
我们永远都是好朋友。

6. A friend is never known till a man has need.
不到患难时，永远不能认识真正的朋友。

7. You are the real friend who walks in when the rest of the world walks out.
谢谢你是那位全世界都遗弃我时还在我身边的朋友。

8. A friend is best found in adversity.
患难见真友。

读书笔记

22 Old Friends 老朋友

Old friends, they finish your sentences, they remember the cat that ran away when you were twelve, and they tell you the truth when you've had a bad **haircut**. But mostly, they are always there for you—whether it's in person or via late night phone calls—through good times and bad. But as the years pass, it becomes **increasingly** difficult to see each other, to make new memories. Fortunately, my high school girlfriends and I **vowed** long ago not to let this happen. We vowed to have **reunions**.

老朋友，他们会接完你没说完的句子，他们记得在你十二岁时跑掉的那只猫，如果你剪了一个很糟糕的发型，他们会跟你说实话。但主要的是，不论是在美好或糟糕的日子里，他们总会在你身边——或是面对面交流，或是深夜与你通电话。但是随着年月流逝，彼此越来越难见到对方，也越来越难制造新的回忆了。幸运的是，很早以前，我与我的一帮高中女友们曾立下誓言不让这样的事发生，我们许诺一定要重聚。

A few months ago, we met up for a three-day weekend in the American southwest. We grew up together in Maine and have said for years that we should have an annual event. Yet it's often postponed or canceled due to schedule conflicts. Not this year.

几个月前的一个周末，我们在美国西南部聚了三天。我们一起在缅因州长大，这几年来一直都在说我们应该有个一年一度的聚会，但通常都因为日程计划冲突而延迟或取消。今年终于如愿了。

Four of us—two from San Francisco, one from Boston, and one from Seattle—boarded planes bound for Santa Fe, New Mexico, where one of the gang lives and works for an art gallery. Two years ago, she moved there—escaped, rather—

我们一行四人——两个来自旧金山，一个来自波士顿，还有一个来自西雅图——登上了飞往新墨西哥州圣菲的航班。我们这帮人中有一个住在圣菲，为那里的一家画廊工作。

from the film industry in New York city, where she led a life that felt too fast, too unfulfilling. The artist in her longed for vibrant landscapes and starry moonlit skies. She wanted to drive a truck on dusty roads, a trusty dog at her side, riding shotgun. She got all that and found love, too. She is happy.

两年前，她搬到那里——更准确地说是从纽约的电影业中逃离出来。她当时觉得在纽约生活节奏太快，太没有成就感。她那艺术家的本性向往生机盎然的自然景致和繁星点缀的月夜。她希望能在尘土飞扬的路上开着卡车，有只忠诚的狗坐在前排的乘客座位，陪伴她左右。这一切都实现了，她还找到了爱情。她是幸福快乐的。

The rest of us—still big city folks—converged on her like a **cyclone** straight out of the pages of a girlfriend novel. Chattering and memory swapping, we were fifteen again in a space of five minutes. Naturally, we relived some of the stories of our youth—angst and all—but we also brought much more to the **gathering** this time. We were new people. We were wives and girlfriends to someone back home. We were business women, artists and writers. We were no longer girls, no longer postcollege grads. We were women.

我们其余几人——仍然是大城市居民——像是从女性小说的页面中直接跳出来的一股旋风似地向她袭去。我们聊天、分享回忆，仿佛在短短的五分钟内又重返十五岁。我们自然而然地重温了年轻时候的故事——忧愁、怅惘等种种情感——但我们给这次聚会带来的还不止这些。我们是有着全新身份的人，我们是家里那位的妻子或女友，我们是女商人、艺术家及作家，我们不再是小女孩，也不再是刚毕业的大学生，我们已成为女人。

I shared an air mattress that night with my friend from Boston, the one who calls me, while **rubbernecking** in traffic, to catch up on her cell phone, to tell me of her life and love. On the next mattress was a gal from San Francisco, newly single and enjoying

那天晚上，我与来自波士顿的朋友共睡一张充气床。路上交通堵塞时，她会边看热闹边给我打电话闲聊，说说她的生活及爱情。旁边的另一张床上睡的是来自旧金山的朋友，她刚刚恢复单身，正享受着一个人的生

her independence. Our host, the artist, shared her bedroom that weekend with a married dot-commer from San Francisco. Yes, we are different, but we are also the same. The years of our youth say so.

活。我们的主人—那位艺术家，那个周末与来自旧金山，就职IT行业的一位已婚姐妹同住一间房。是的，我们变得不同了，但我们又仍然未变。我们的青春岁月可以证明这一切。

单词解析 *Word Analysis*

haircut ['heəkʌt] *n.* 理发

例 Your hair is all right; it's just that you need a haircut.
你的头发还好；不过你该理发了。

increasingly [ɪn'kriːsɪŋli] *adv.* 渐增地，越来越多地

例 He was finding it increasingly difficult to make decisions.
他发现越来越难以做出决定。

vow [vaʊ] *v.* 发誓，立誓

例 I solemnly vowed that someday I would return to live in Europe.
我郑重发誓，总有一天我将回到欧洲生活。

reunion [riː'juːniən] *n.* 团聚，重聚，聚会

例 The whole family was there for this big family reunion.
全家人都来参加了这次盛大的家庭聚会。

cyclone ['saɪkləʊn] *n.* 龙卷风，旋风

例 A cyclone in the Bay of Bengal is threatening the eastern Indian states.
发生在孟加拉湾的飓风正威胁着印度东部各邦。

gathering ['gæðərɪŋ] *n.* 聚会，集会

例 He called on Mr. White to speak at the gathering.
他请怀特先生在集会上讲话。

rubberneck ['rʌbənek] v. 伸长脖子看，好奇地听

例 The accident was caused by people slowing down to rubber-neck.
事故是因为看热闹而减速的人而引起的。

语法知识点 *Grammar Points*

① Yet it's often postponed or canceled due to schedule conflicts.

due to 由于，因为

例 Mistakes due to carelessness may have serious consequences.
由粗心大意造成的错误有可能带来严重的后果。

due to+n.（名词）/doing sth. 解释为由……导致

例 The accident was due to careless driving.
这次车祸起因于驾驶疏忽。

due to、because of与owing to都是表原因的词语，但是三者在用法上还是有所不同的：

due to 解释为由于、因……造成，在句中除了可做状语之外还可以做表语或者定语，在做状语的时候不能用于句首。作表语和状语时与owing to意义相同。

例 Your failure is due to negligence.
你的失败是由于疏忽造成的。

because of 解释为"因为、由于"，在句中通常作状语。because of后面可以加n.（名词）、pron.（代词）、ppl.（分词）和what引导的名词性从句，在句中与其他成分不用逗号隔开，是非常口语化的表达方式。

例 Because of his bad leg, he couldn't walk so fast as others.
由于他的腿坏了，他不能像其他人走得那么快。

owing to 解释为"由于、因为、多亏"，在句中作状语和表语，作状语时习惯用逗号将其和句子其他成分分开。owing to与because of一样，强调因果关系。

例 They decided to cancel the flight, owing to the storm.
由于这场暴风雨，他们决定取消这个航班。

② The artist in her longed for vibrant landscapes and starry moonlit skies.

longed for 久盼的，渴望许久的

例 This is a much longed-for holiday for children.
对于孩子们来说这是一次渴望已久的假期。

例 It is never late to start striving towards the longed-for objectives.
为自己向往的目标奋斗，无论何时起都不算晚。

③ Chattering and memory swapping, we were fifteen again in a space of five minutes.

chattering and memory swapping 为现在分词作伴随状语

伴随状语的逻辑主语一般情况下必须是全句的主语，伴随状语与谓语动词所表示的动作或状态是同时发生的。伴随状语首先是一种状语，用来修饰动词，同时表示与谓语动词同时进行，即伴随着谓语动词的动作同时进行。

例 He said it angrily pointing at the notice on the wall.
他生气地说着，手指着墙上的布告。

例 The dog entered the room, following his master.
这条狗跟着主人进了屋。

经典名句 *Famous Classics*

1. Friendship—one soul in two bodies.
友谊是两人一条心。

2. A good book is a best friend who never turns his back upon us.
一本好书，莫逆之交。

3. Our friendship is constant.
我们的友谊永不变。

4. Admonish your friends in private; praise them in public.
在私底下要忠告你的朋友，在公开场合要表扬你的朋友。

5. We can live without our friends, but not without our neighbours.
生活可无友，邻居不能无。

6. A friend is not so soon gotten as lost.
交友慢，失友快。

23 Eight Types of Friends (I)
八种类型的朋友（Ⅰ）

Did you know that people without friends are more likely to die an early death?

你知道吗？没有朋友的人往往死得早。

It's true. Just ask science.

这是真的，不信，可以向科学求证。

To up your chances of living a long, happy life, having a bunch of **fair-weather** buddies won't do the trick. You need a **diverse**, well-rounded **entourage** that will stick with you through thick and thin. The following eight types of friends are just what you need to keep the doctor away.

要想生活得长久幸福，一群不能共患难的朋友是不能助你达成目的的。你需要的是一群性格各异、面面俱到、可以与你同甘苦共患难的朋友。接下来要说的八种类型的朋友正是这一类。

1. A Loyal Best Friend

1. 一个忠实的最好的朋友

Sometimes a loyal best friend is the only thing you need to stay **sane**. Everyone needs a non-judgmental friend who will support them no matter what. This is the kind of friend who lets you be a hot mess and knows all of your deepest and darkest secrets, but still loves you all the same.

有时一个忠实的最好的朋友可以是使你保持清醒的唯一原因。每个人都需要一个无论在任何情况下都无私支持自己的朋友，这样的朋友可以放任你的一团糟，也知道你所有的最深处和最黑暗的秘密，但仍然一直爱着你。

2. A Fearless Adventurer

2. 一个无所畏惧的冒险者

We live in a big world where there are so many places to see, people to meet, and experiences to be had, yet so many of us are stuck in our own **routines** and forget to, well, live. We all need an **adventurous** friend who will pull us out of our shells and introduce

我们生活在一个宏大的世界里，可以看许多风景，遇到各色的人，拥有丰富多彩的经历。然而，我们大部分人都深陷在自己的琐事里，忘记如何好好地生活。我们都需要一个爱冒险的朋友，将自己从壳里

us to new ideas, cultures, philosophies, and activities.

3. A Brutally Honest Confidant

There's certain situations in life where we need to hear the harsh truth. That's what the **brutally** honest confidant is for. If you're in a rocky relationship and everyone's telling you that it's perfectly normal that you're back with that special someone for the 8th time in the last 2 years, the brutally honest confidant is there to **yank** your rose-colored glasses off and tell you, "Enough. Stop with all that break-up-and-get-back-together drama. You deserve better." Friends are supposed to be honest with each other. If you find someone who is brutally honest with you (in a constructive way), then hold on to this person! People like that are hard to come by these days.

4. A Wise Mentor

The wise **mentor** in your life doesn't have to be someone who shares the same **occupation** or hobbies with you. It's simply someone who's a few steps ahead of you in life and has enough wisdom and patience to guide you in the right direction. It can be anyone—a colleague, a friend who's beyond their years, or an older neighbor—as long as you look up to this person and want to be more like them.

拖出来并向我们介绍新想法、文化、哲学和活动。

3. 一个极其诚实的知己

在生活中，有些特定的场合，我们需要知道残酷的真相。这时我们正需要这样一个极其诚实的知己。在一段摇摆不定的恋爱关系中，每个人都对你说情人间难免有摩擦，你应该再次回到那个人身边，而这已是过去两年里第八次出现。此时那个极其诚实的知己则会摘掉你乐观的眼镜，对你说，“够了！不要再上演那种分分合合的戏码了。你值得更好的人”。朋友之间应该相互坦诚。如果你发现某个人对你极其诚实（以一种建设性的方式），那么就紧紧抓住这个人。在这个时代，像这样的人已经不多了。

4. 一位睿智的导师

在你的生命中，一位睿智的导师不一定要是某个职位与你相同的或是拥有共同爱好的人。仅仅是某个生活阅历比你多点儿，拥有足够智慧和能力，可以指引你走向正确方向的人。他可以是任何人——一位同事、一个阅历丰富的朋友或是一位年老的邻居，只要你敬仰并且想要成为甚至超越他们。

单词解析 Word Analysis

fair-weather ['feə,weðə] *adj.* 同甘不共苦的，只在顺境中的

例 He has realized that Bill is a fair-weather friend.
他已意识到比尔是个不能共患难的朋友。

diverse [daɪ'vɜːs] *adj.* 各式各样的，形形色色的

例 Society is now much more diverse than ever before.
当今社会较之以往任何时候都要丰富多彩得多。

entourage ['ɒnturaːʒ] *n.* 随从人员

例 He was accompanied by an entourage of a dozen police officers.
他有12名警官随行。

sane [seɪn] *adj.* 心智健全的，神志清醒的

例 It wasn't the act of a sane person.
心智健全的人做不出这种事来。

routine [ruː'tiːn] *n.* 常规，惯例，例行公事

例 The players had to change their daily routine and lifestyle.
这些运动员不得不改变他们的日常生活习惯和方式。

adventurous [əd'ventʃərəs] *adj.* 爱冒险的，敢于创新的

例 Warren was an adventurous businessman.
沃伦是个敢于冒险的商人。

brutally ['bruːtəlɪ] *adv.* 残忍的，野蛮的

例 The writing is brutally tough and savagely humorous.
该作品带有残酷的强悍和野性的幽默感。

yank [jæŋk] *v.* 猛拉，猛拽

例 She yanked the child back into the house.
她使劲儿把那个孩子拽回了房子里。

mentor ['mentɔː(r)] *n.* 指导者，导师

例 He has really a bit of a mentor for me.
他真的有点儿像我的导师。

occupation [ˌɒkju'peɪʃn] *n.* 职业

例 I suppose I was looking for an occupation which was going to be an adventure.
我想我在找的是一份具有冒险性的工作。

语法知识点 *Grammar Points*

① Did you know that people without friends are more likely to die an early death?

be more likely to 更可能，更容易

例 If you provide them with the information they need, they will be more likely to buy from you.
如果你向他们提供他们需要的信息，他们将更有可能购买你。

例 Yes, if we are always things each time, then it would be more likely to trouble.
是，如果我们每一次总是就事论事的话，可能会比较麻烦。

② Friends are supposed to be honest with each other.

be supposed to 应该，被期望，to是动词不定式符号，其后要跟动词原形。

当be supposed to...的主语是“人”时，意为“应该……”“被期望……”，它可以用来表示劝告、建议、义务、责任等，相当于情态动词should。

例 Everyone is supposed to wear a seat-belt in the car.
每个人在汽车里都应该系安全带。

当be supposed to...的主语是“物”时，它表示“本应，本该”，用于表示“某事本应该发生而没有发生”。

例 The train was supposed to arrive half an hour ago.
火车本应在半小时之前到达。

③ It can be anyone—a colleague, a friend who's beyond their years, or an older neighbor—as long as you look up to this person and want to be more like them.

as long as 可以表达4种含义：长达，达……之久；当……时候；既然，由于，因为；只要，在……情形下，在本文中表达的是最后一个含义。

例 The wall is as long as that one.
这道墙与那道墙一样长。

例 She tried to stay awake for as long as she could.
她尽量不让自己睡去，能醒多久就醒多久。

例 The fruit should be left on the tree as long as possible.
水果应该尽可能留在树上长久一些。

经典名句 *Famous Classics*

1. Friendship is indispensable to people's life.
友谊是人们生活中不可缺少的一部分。

2. Friendship cannot stand always on one side.
来而不往非礼也。

3. Be slow in choosing a friend; slower in changing.
选择朋友要审慎，改换更要审又慎。

4. God defend me from my friends; from my enemy I can defend myself.
防友靠天，防敌靠己。

5. Life without a friend is death without a witness.
在世无朋友，死后无证人。

6. A friend is a second self.
朋友是另一个我。

7. God helps those who help themselves.
自助者天助之。

24 Eight Types of Friends (II) 八种类型的朋友（Ⅱ）

5. A Friend from a Different Culture

Being in a cross-cultural friendship allows you to explore customs, values, and **traditions** outside of your own culture. Sometimes you might even adopt new ways to do things. Be careful: don't **befriend** someone just because they're from a different culture. No one likes to be a **token** friend. Instead, keep your mind open, and if you come across someone you click with who just so happens to be from a different culture, make the effort to learn about their customs, values, and traditions while getting to know the person on a personal level.

5. 来自不同文化的朋友

一段跨文化的友谊可以使你体验与自己文化迥然不同的习俗、价值观和传统。有时，你甚至可能采用新的方式做事。注意，不要就因为某人来自不同文化就与其成为朋友，没人喜欢成为象征性的朋友。相反，你要敞开心胸。如果你在网上遇到某个人恰巧来自不同的文化，要努力去了解他们的习俗、价值观念和传统，同时从个人的层面去了解这个人。

6. A Polar Opposite

Instead of **constantly** surrounding yourself with like-minded people, try to break out of your comfort zone and befriend people who hold **opposing** views. They will help open your eyes to different world views and you'll learn to accept people who don't see the world exactly the way you see it.

6. 一个完全对立的朋友

除了不断地使志同道合的人围绕在身边，你应该试着打破这种安逸，同观点与你对立的人做朋友。他们可以帮助你拓展不同世界观的视野，而你也将学会接受以一种迥异于你的方式看待世界的人。

7. A Friendly Neighbor

These days, a lot of people don't know their own neighbors. It's a shame,

7. 一位友好的邻居

这些年，很多人不了解自己的邻居，这真是羞愧。因为

because some neighbors can be the nicest and most helpful people ever. If you're on a vacation, and you suddenly realize that you forgot to lock the front door, you can call up your trusty of neighbor and ask them to head over to your house and lock it for you. Nice **dependable** neighbors who have each other's backs are a dying breed, but that doesn't mean you shouldn't introduce yourself to the new neighbors across the street!

一些邻居可以成为最友好和最热心的人。要是你正在度假，突然意识到自己忘记锁大门了，你可以打电话给信任的邻居，让他们前去你家，帮你锁好大门。拥有友好并相互照应的邻居是千金难买，但那并不意味着你不应该向街对面的新邻居介绍你自己。

8. A Work Pal

Did you know that with a full-time job, you spend at least 50% of your waking hours at work? Not only that, but you spend some more time commuting to work, thinking about work, working overtime, and furthering your career on your personal time. **Depressing**, isn't it?

Statistics show that the more **isolated** you are at work, the more depressed you get. That's why it makes sense to get a work pal to chat with at the water cooler and to help you get through the week. You spend 50% of your waking hours at work, and so does your work pal. You'll find it much easier to shoot the breeze and complain about work with someone who can relate to you than eating lunch alone every day.

8. 一位工作伙伴

你知道吗？在拥有一份全职工作后，你至少花费了50%醒着的时间在工作上。不仅仅是那样，你还要多花费些时间在通勤、思考工作、加班，还要在个人时间上拓展事业。真令人沮丧，是不是？

数据表明，在工作上越孤立，你就变得越抑郁。这就是为什么需要一个可以在饮水机旁聊天并且助你度过一周的工作伙伴。你花50%醒着的时间在工作上，你的工作伙伴也一样。与每天独自吃午饭相比，你会发现与合得来的人闲聊或是抱怨工作是更容易的事。

一生中，有一个忠实的最好的朋友、一个无所畏惧的冒险者、一位极其诚实的知己、

With a loyal best friend, a **fearless** adventurer, a brutally honest confidant, a wise mentor, a friend from a different culture, a polar opposite, a friendly neighbor, and a work pal in your life, you're bound to live a long and happy life!

一位睿智的导师、一个来自不同文化的朋友、一个完全对立的朋友、一个友好的邻居以及一个工作伙伴，你必将活得长久而快乐。

单词解析 *Word Analysis*

tradition [trə'dɪʃn] *n.* 传统，传说

例 Mary has carried on the family tradition of giving away plants.
玛丽承袭了向别人赠送植物的家族传统。

befriend [bɪ'frend] *v.* 交朋友；把……当朋友

例 The film's about an elderly woman and a young nurse who befriends her.
电影讲述的是一位老太太和一个待她友善的年轻护士的故事。

token ['təʊkən] *adj.* 象征性的，装点门面的

例 Miners have staged a two-hour token stoppage to demand better pay and conditions.
矿工们举行了两小时的象征性停工，以要求提高工资和改善工作条件。

constantly ['kɒnstəntli] *adv.* 不断地，时常地

例 We are constantly being reminded to cut down our fat intake.
不断有人提醒我们要减少脂肪的摄入量。

opposing [ə'pəʊzɪŋ] *adj.* 对立的，截然相反的

例 Water is the opposing force to fire.
水火不相容。

isolated ['aɪsəleɪtɪd] *adj.* 孤独的，隔离的

例 Aubrey's family's farm is very isolated.
奥布里家的农场非常偏僻。

depressing [dɪ'presɪŋ] adj. 令人沮丧的

例 Yesterday's unemployment figures were depressing.
昨天的失业数字令人沮丧。

fearless ['fɪələs] adj. 无畏的，不怕的

例 The soldiers followed their fearless leader into the battle.
士兵们随着他们勇敢的指挥官投入战斗。

语法知识点 *Grammar Points*

① if you come across someone you click with who just so happens to be from a different culture, make the effort to learn about.

come across 碰巧遇见，相当于run across，上文中是此意

例 I've just come across a beautiful poem in this book.
我在这本书里偶然发现一首优美的诗。

come across 还可以表示被理解，被传达；使人产生某种印象

例 He spoke for a long time but his meaning did not really come across.
他讲了很长时间，但他的意思没有人真正理解。

例 Your speech came across very well.
你的演说相当受欢迎。

② If you're on a vacation, and you suddenly realize that you forgot to lock the front door, you can call up your trusty of neighbor.

on a vacation 在度假

例 On a vacation at home, Louis, age 15, picked up a blunt awl.
在家中度假的一天，15岁的路易斯捡起了一把钝锥子。

例 But suppose you go on a vacation to the Caribbean instead.
但是假设你去加勒比海度假了。

③ That's why it makes sense to get a work pal to chat with at the water cooler and to help you get through the week.

make sense 讲得通，有意义；是明智的，是合情合理的

最常见的用法是“没有道理”：doesn’t make sense; doesn’t make any sense

例 The movie doesn’t make any sense.
这个电影根本就是瞎编。

例 It still doesn’t make sense to me.
我还是没明白。

经典名句 *Famous Classics*

1. A man’s best friends are his ten fingers.
人最好的朋友是自己的十个手指。

2. Only they who fulfill their duties in everyday matters will fulfill them on great occasions.
只有在日常生活中尽责的人才会在重大时刻尽责。

3. The shortest way to do many things is to do only one thing at a time.
做许多事情的捷径就是一次只做一件事。

4. One never lose anything by politeness.
讲礼貌不吃亏。

5. There’s only one corner of the universe you can be sure of improving, and that’s your own self.
这个宇宙中只有一个角落你肯定可以改进，那就是你自己。

6. The world is like a mirror: Frown at it and it frowns at you; smile, and it smiles too.
世界犹如一面镜子：朝它皱眉它就朝你皱眉，朝它微笑它也朝你微笑。

7. Death comes to all, but great achievements raise a monument which shall endure until the sun grows old.
死亡无人能免，但非凡的成就会树起一座纪念碑，它将一直立到太阳冷却之时。

25 Help from Friends 来自朋友的帮忙

The day my fiancé fell to his death, it started to snow, just like any November day, just like the bottom hadn't fallen out of my world when he fell off the roof. His body, when I found it, was lightly covered with snow. It snowed almost every day for the next four months, while I sat on the couch and watched it pile up.

One morning, I shuffled **downstairs** and was startled to see a **snowplow** clearing my driveway and the bent back of a woman shoveling my walk. I dropped to my knees, crawled through the living room, and back upstairs so those good **Samaritans** would not see me. I was mortified. My first thought was how would I ever repay them? I didn't have the strength to brush my hair let alone shovel someone's walk.

Before Jon's death, I took pride in the fact that I rarely asked for help or favors. I defined myself by my **competence** and **independence**. so who was I if I was no longer capable and busy? How could I respect myself if all I did was sit on the couch everyday and watch the snow fall?

我未婚夫去世的那天，天开始下雪，就仿佛是十一月某个普通的一天，就仿佛当他从房顶上跌下时，我的世界并没有垮塌。当我发现他时，他的身体上已经盖上了一层薄薄的雪。之后的四个月，差不多每个月都在下雪，而我就坐在沙发上，看着雪一点点堆积起来。

一天早上，我慢吞吞地下楼，却吃惊地发现一台扫雪机正在清扫我的车道，还有一个女人正弯腰铲去走道上的雪。我感到十分羞愧。为了不让外面的好心人看到，我跪在地上，爬着穿过客厅，回到楼上。我首先想到的就是，怎样才能回报他们？我情绪低落得连梳头的力气都没，更别说帮别人铲雪了。

乔恩去世之前，我把自己定位成一个独立的、能干的人，我因此为很少请求别人的帮助和关心而自豪。如果我不再忙碌，不再能干，那么我是谁？如果我整天蜷在沙发上看着窗外飘落的雪花，我拿什么获得自尊？

Learning how to receive the love and support that came my way wasn't easy. Friends cooked for me and I cried because I couldn't even help them set the table. "I'm not usually this lazy," I wailed. Finally, my friend Kathy sat down with me and said, "Mary, cooking for you is not a **chore**. I love you and I want to do it. It makes me feel good to be able to do something for you."

学习接受别人的爱和帮助并不简单。朋友们为我做饭，我哭了，因为我甚至不能帮他们摆餐具。“我通常不是这样懒惰的。”我哀泣道。后来，我朋友凯茜坐在我旁边，安慰我说：“玛丽，为你做饭并不是个负担。我爱你，我很愿意为你做饭，能够帮上忙让我感觉很好。”

Over and over, I heard similar **sentiments** from the people who supported me during those dark days. One very wise man told me, "You are not doing nothing. Being fully open to your grief may be the hardest work you will ever do."

那些帮助我度过人生中的黑暗时刻的人们，一次又一次地用充满感情的话来安慰我。一个很睿智的人告诉过我：“你并不是无所事事，完全地无保留地直面痛苦，可能是最难做的事。”

I am not the person I once was, but in many ways I have changed for the better. The **fabric** of my life is now woven with gratitude and **humility**. I have been surprised to learn that there is incredible freedom that comes from facing one's worst fear and walking away whole. I believe there is strength in surrender.

我已经不是以前的我，很多方面我已变得更好了。现在，我生命的锦缎是由感恩和谦恭织成的。我很惊奇地了解到，当你面对自己最痛苦的、最可怕的经历，坚强地挺过来，你会感受到难以置信的自由。我相信当你直面现实，你会获得力量。

单词解析 *Word Analysis*

downstairs [ˌdaʊnˈsteəz] *adv.* 往楼下，顺楼梯而下

例 Denise went downstairs and made some tea.
丹尼丝下楼泡了茶。

snowplow ['snəʊˌplaʊ] *n.* 扫雪车

例 With the development and progress of society, the demand of snowplow is more and more in China.

随着社会的发展和进步，国内对除雪装置的需求越来越高。

Samaritans [sə'mæritənz] *n.* (在别人危难时予以帮助的)撒马利亚人；助人为乐者

例 A good Samaritan offered us a room in his house.

一个好心人让我们住在他家的一间房里。

competence ['kɒmpɪtəns] *n.* 能力

例 We've always regarded him as a man of integrity and high professional competence.

我们一直都认为他是个正直而且业务能力很强的人。

independence [ˌɪndɪ'pendəns] *n.* 独立，自主

例 In 1816, Argentina declared its independence from Spain.

1816年，阿根廷宣布脱离西班牙正式独立。

chore [tʃɔː(r)] *n.* 杂事，琐事

例 She sees exercise primarily as an unavoidable chore.

她基本上把锻炼看作是不得不做的琐事。

sentiment ['sentɪmənt] *n.* 态度，情绪

例 Public sentiment rapidly turned anti-American.

公众情绪迅速转变，开始反对美国。

fabric ['fæbrɪk] *n.* 织物，布料

例 Whatever your colour scheme, there's a fabric to match.

无论什么样的色彩图案，都有与之相配的织物。

humility [hjuː'mɪləti] *n.* 谦逊，谦恭

例 For a long time he still thought like a millionaire but he has humility now.

在很长一段时间里，他仍以一个百万富翁的方式思维，但他现在变得谦恭了。

语法知识点 *Grammar Points*

① The day my fiancé fell to his death, it started to snow, just like any November day, just like the bottom hadn't fallen out of my world when he fell off the roof.

fall to death 摔死

例 Almost invariably they get crushed to death, freeze to death or fall to death.
几乎无一例外，他们被踩死，冻死或跌倒死亡。

例 Suppose that as a child, you saw someone fall to their death from a roller coaster.
假设你在童年时代曾目睹有人从过山车上坠落而死的悲剧。

just like 正像

例 You mean he sent you back just like that?
你是说他就那样把你打发回来了?

例 You should have told us. But it's just like you never share.
你应该早告诉我们的。不过你就是这么个人，把事情都藏在心里。

fall out of 是个常用短语，意思是"放弃，中止……"等。例如：fall out of use 的意思就是"不再被使用，被淘汰"。

例 The area fell out of habitation for lack of water.
那地方因缺水已无人居住。

fall of 跌落、从……掉下来，后直接接宾语（相当于fall down from...）

例 They spread a big net in case Tom should fall off the tree and get hurt.
他们支开一张大网以防汤姆从树上掉下来受伤。

② I didn't have the strength to brush my hair let alone shovel someone's walk.

let alone （通常用在否定句后）更别提，更不用说

例 He did not have enough money to have the tire patched up, let alone buy a new one.
他的钱还不够补这个轮胎，更别提买个新的了。

not to mention和let alone含义基本相同，用法存在细微差别，not to mention后面只接名词性短语，let alone后面可接任何词性的词项。

③ Before Jon's death, I took pride in the fact that I rarely asked for help or favors. I defined myself by my competence and independence.

take pride in 以……自豪，对……感到满意

例 We take pride in offering you the highest standards.
我们为向您提供最高标准的服务而感到自豪。

经典名句 *Famous Classics*

1. Understanding, love and tolerance are the first three essences that comes to an authentic friendship.
理解、爱和容忍是一份真正友谊所需的最重要的3个品质。

2. It takes many special qualities to make a friend. Understanding should come first.
结交朋友需要具备很多专门的品质。首先是理解。

3. Friendship multiplies joys and divides grieves.
友谊可以增添欢乐，可以分担忧愁。

4. Books, like friends, should be few and well chosen.
书籍如朋友，应该少而精。

读书笔记

26 A Friend's Pray 朋友的祈祷

A voyaging ship was **wrecked** during a storm at sea and only two of the men aboard were able to swim to a small, desert-like island. Not knowing what else to do, the two survivors agreed that they had no other recourse than to pray to God.

一艘客轮在海上遇到暴风雨而翻覆，只有两个人靠游泳到了一个荒凉的小岛上。在无计可施的情况下，这两个人都认为只有向上帝祷告才是唯一之道。

However, to find out whose prayers were more powerful, they agreed to divide the **territory** between them and stay on **opposite** sides of the island.

但是为了看谁的祷告比较有效，他们协议把小岛分成两半，每人各居一处。

The first thing they prayed for was food. The next morning, the first man saw a fruit-bearing tree on his side of the island, and he was able to eat its fruit. But the other man's **parcel** of land remained **barren**.

他们祈祷的第一件事就是食物，第二天早上，第一个人看到一棵果实累累的果树长在他这一边的土地上，现在他就有果子可以吃了。而另外一个人的土地上依旧一片荒芜。

After a week, the first man became **lonely** and decided to pray for a wife. The next day, another ship was wrecked and the only survivor was a woman who swam to his side of the island. But on the other side of the island, there was nothing.

一个星期以后，第一个人感到很孤单寂寞，所以他决定祈求能有一个妻子。第二天，又有一艘船失事了，唯一幸存的女人游泳到他这一边的岛上来。而另一边的岛上则什么也没有。

Soon thereafter the first man prayed for a house, clothes and more food. The next day, like magic, all of these things were given to him. However, the second

不久，第一个人又祈求得到一间房子、衣服和更多的食物。隔天，他所祈求的东西就像变魔术一样全都出现了，而

man still had nothing.

Finally, the first man prayed for a ship so that he and his wife could leave the island, and in the morning he found a ship **docked** at his side of the island.

The first man boarded the ship with his wife and decided to leave the second man on the island, considering the other man **unworthy** to receive God's blessings since none of his prayers had been answered.

As the ship was about to leave, the first man heard a voice from Heaven booming, "Why are you leaving your companion on the island?"

"My blessings are mine alone since I was the one who prayed for them," the first man answered. "His prayers were all unanswered and so he doesn't deserve anything."

"You are mistaken!" the voice **rebuked** him. "He had only one **prayer**, which I answered. If not for that, you would not have received any of my blessings."

"Tell me," the first man asked the voice, "What did he pray for that I should owe him anything?"

"He prayed that all your prayers would be answered."

另一个人还是什么都没有。

最后，第一个人祈求能有一艘船，让他跟他的妻子可以离开小岛。早上醒来，他看到一艘船就停泊在他这里的岸边。

第一个人和他太太上了船，他决定把第二个人留在那个小岛上。他认为另一个人不值得得到上帝的恩赐，因为他的祈祷一个也没应验。

正当船要离开的时候，第一个人听到天上传来轰隆的声音说：“为什么你把你的同伴留在岛上？”

第一个人回答说：“上帝的赐予都归我独享，因为是我祈求而来的。他的祈祷全都没应验，所以他不配得到任何东西。”

“你错了！”那个声音责备他说：“我应允了他唯一的一个祈求，若非如此，你根本得不到我任何的赐予。”

“告诉我。”第一个人问那个声音说：“他到底祈求什么，使我对他有所亏欠？”

“他祈祷让你的祈求都能应验。”

单词解析 Word Analysis

wreck [rek] *v.* 破坏，毁坏，损坏

例 A coalition could have defeated the government and wrecked the treaty.
联盟本来可以击败政府并毁掉该条约的。

territory ['terətri] *n.* 领土，土地

例 The government denies that any of its territory is under rebel control.
政府否认有领土被反叛分子所控制。

opposite ['ɒpəzɪt] *adj.* 完全相反的

例 I should have written the notes in the opposite order.
我本应按相反的顺序记笔记的。

parcel ['pɑːsl] *n.* 包裹

例 He had a large brown paper parcel under his left arm.
他左臂下夹着一个大牛皮纸邮包。

barren ['bærən] *adj.* 荒芜的，缺少植被的

例 He wants to use the water to irrigate barren desert land.
他想用这些水灌溉荒漠。

lonely ['ləʊnli] *adj.* 孤单的，孤独的

例 I desperately needed something to occupy me during those long, lonely nights.
在那一个个漫长、孤单的夜晚，我亟须找点事做。

dock [dɒk] *v.* （船）靠码头

例 The vessel docked at Liverpool in April 1811.
这艘轮船于1811年4月在利物浦靠岸。

unworthy [ʌn'wɜːði] *adj.* 不值得的

例 You may feel unworthy of the attention and help people offer you.
你可能会觉得自己不值得别人关心和帮助。

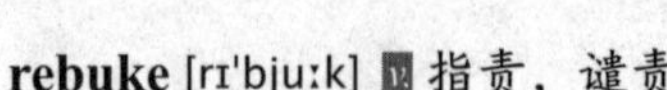

rebuke [rɪ'bjuːk] *v.* 指责，谴责

例 The president rebuked the House and Senate for not passing those bills within 100 days.

总统谴责参众两院没有在100天之内通过那些法案。

prayer [preə(r)] *n.* 祈祷，祷告

例 They joined a religious order and dedicated their lives to prayer and good works.

他们加入了一个宗教团体，终生都将祈祷和行善。

语法知识点 *Grammar Points*

① Not knowing what else to do, the two survivors agreed that they had no other recourse than to pray to God.

no other...than 除了……之外，没有……。该短语中间加名词，相当于no...other than，这两种形式表达同一种意思。

例 We can think of no other example than this.

除了这个例子以外，我们想不出别的来了。

例 No fuels other than petroleum will be fit for this purpose.

除石油外其他燃料都将不适于这种用途。

② ...the first man prayed for a ship so that he and his wife could leave the island...

英语中，结果状语从句和目的状语从句都有so that，但是不一样：结果状语从句中是“so...that...”，so 和 that 是分开的；目的状语从句中是“... so that ...”，so that 之间只有一个空格。

例 She is so pretty that everyone around her likes her.

她是如此的美丽，以至于她周围的人都很喜欢她。

例 She spoke gently so that he would not be too excited.

她轻声细语地给他说，为的是不让他过于激动。

在使用的时候，有时候会出现“such...that...”结构，这个结构和so...that...结构的区别在于：so是个副词，而such是个形容词，这样so后面接形容词或副词，such后面则接名词或名词短语。

经典名句 Famous Classics

1. The reason why a great man is great is that he resolves to be a great man.
伟人之所以伟大，是因为他立志要成为伟大的人。

2. Suffering is the most powerful teacher of life.
苦难是人生最伟大的老师。

3. Pencil and a dream can take you anywhere.
拿起笔，写下你的梦想，你的人生就从此刻起航！

4. It is during our darkest moments that we must focus to see the light.
越是在艰难困苦的时候，我们越是要看到希望。

5. Judge each day not by the harvest you reap but by the seeds you plant.
不要问自己收获了多少果实，而是要问自己今天播种了多少种子。

6. The best way out is always through.
一路走到底，你就会发现那个最佳出口。

7. The questions you ask determine the quality of your life.
你生活的品质取决于你所提出的问题。

8. Believe you can and you're halfway there.
相信自己，你就成功了一半。

读书笔记

27 Difference between Friendship and Love 友情和爱情的区别

Both are so much related to each other. And both are so **dissimilar**! What are the differences between friendship and love? Is platonic friendship possible between persons of opposite sex? Let us try and understand.

两者联系是如此密切，两者却又那么截然不同。友情和爱情有什么区别？异性朋友间的理想化的友谊真的存在吗？我们来试着理解下。

What is friendship? Why do we call a person our friend? When do we call someone a very good friend? If we care for a person, if we are always ready to help that person and if we share most of our thoughts with a person, they are our good friends. We can always count upon our good friends in an emergency. We are always sure that our friend will understand why we acted in a certain way. We need not explain anything to our very good friends. The friendship is so deep and the relationship is so **intimate**, that most of the things are **automatically** understood by our friends.

什么是友情？为什么我们管一个人叫“朋友”？什么时候我们管一个人叫作“好朋友”？如果我们关心一个人，我们总是准备帮助那个人；如果我们和某个人分享大部分的想法，那个人一定是我们的好朋友。在紧急情况下我们总是依靠好朋友。我们总是确定好友会理解我们的行事方式。我们不需要向亲密的朋友解释什么。友情如此深，关系如此牢，以至于朋友间的事双方都会很自然地理解。

What about love? In a relationship of deep love, all the sharing that we discussed above are taken for granted. But love **transcends** all this. During love, we are attached with a particular person, while in friendship, one may have many friends. A loving relationship makes one

什么是爱情？在深爱的关系中，上面我们讨论的事情都是理所当然的。但是爱情远远超过这些。恋爱中，我们总是和某一个人关系密切。但是在友情中，一个人可能有很多朋友。恋爱的两个人联系得如此紧密，如果他/她受到了伤害，

so much **attached** to the other, that one gets pained if his/her beloved is hurt! Love also involves a physical element. Friendship does not have that. This is a **vital** difference. Nature gives us love so that the specie can go forward. Nature does not give us friendship.

另一个人也会心痛。爱情总会有身体上的接触。友情却没有。这是至关重要的区别。上苍给予了我们爱情，以使种族延续。但是上苍却没有给我们友情。

Your heart beats will never increase in anticipation of meeting your friend. You will not lie **awake** at night thinking about your friend. You will not feel totally lost, if you don't meet your friend for a few days. You will not have dreams in your eyes thinking about your friend. But in love, you will do all this and much more. Indeed, there is no **comparison** between love and friendship.

在盼朋友出现时，你的心跳不会增加；你不会夜不能寐地想着你的朋友；如果几天没见到朋友，你也不会完全迷失；想到朋友时，你的眼中不会有梦想。但是在恋爱中，这一切你都会做而且程度会更深。确实，爱情和友情没有可比性。

单词解析 *Word Analysis*

dissimilar [dɪ'sɪmɪlə(r)] *adj.* 不一样的，不相似的

例 His methods were not dissimilar to those used by Freud.
他的方法和弗洛伊德的并无二致。

intimate ['ɪntɪmət] *adj.* 亲密的，亲切的

例 France has kept the most intimate links with its former African territories.
法国与其前非洲属地一直保持着最密切的联系。

automatically [ˌɔːtə'mætɪklɪ] *adv.* 自动地，无意识地

例 Don't assume your baby automatically needs feeding if she's fretful.
不要想当然地认为你的宝宝一闹就是要吃奶。

transcend [træn'send] v. 超越，超出

例 He could never transcend his resentments and his complexes.
他从来不能把他的怨恨和感情上的症结置之度外。

attach [ə'tætʃ] v. 贴上，附上

例 We attach labels to things before we file them away.
存档前，我们先贴上标签。

vital ['vaɪtl] adj. 必要的，必不可少的，至关重要的

例 The port is vital to supply relief to millions of drought victims.
这个港口对向数百万旱灾灾民提供救援物资是至关重要的。

awake [ə'weɪk] adj. 醒着的，没睡着的

例 I don't stay awake at night worrying about that.
我并没有因为那件事而担心得彻夜不眠。

comparison [kəm'pærɪsn] n. 比较，对照

例 That comparison isn't as wide of the mark as it seems.
那种比较并非像看起来那么离谱。

语法知识点 *Grammar Points*

① If we care for a person, if we are always ready to help that person and if we share most of our thoughts with a person, they are our good friends. We can always count upon our good friends in an emergency.

care for 关心，照顾，喜欢

例 The sick child was well cared for night and day.
那个生病的孩子日夜受到很好的看护。

例 He likes pop; he doesn't care for classic music.
他喜欢流行歌曲，不喜欢古典音乐。

care about 也可表示“关心，担心”，除此之外，还可表示“在意，计较”

例 He doesn't care about his clothes.
他不在意穿着。

count upon 指望，依赖，依靠，相当于count on

例 That was the only thing they could count on.
那是他们唯一依靠的东西。

例 We could count on benevolent understanding.
我们可以指望得到善意的谅解。

② In a relationship of deep love, all the sharing that we discussed above are taken for granted.

be taken for granted 被认为是理所当然的

例 It should not be taken for granted.
不应该把它认为是理所当然的。

③ Your heart beats will never increase in anticipation of meeting your friend.

in anticipation of 一想到，预料，期待

例 I had taken my coat and umbrella in anticipation of rain.
我估计有雨，所以带着外套和伞。

例 People bought in stocks of tinned goods in anticipation of food rationing.
人们预计食品将定量供应所以买进大量罐头食品。

经典名句 *Famous Classics*

1. Change your thoughts and you change your world.
改变你的思想，你就能改变自己的命运。

2. It is by acts and not by ideas that people live.
行动是根本，想法锦上添花。

3. Happiness is not something you postpone for the future; it is something you design for the present.
幸福不应该留到未来品尝，幸福是你专门为当下的自己所准备的。

4. Mankind is made great or little by its own will.
一个人伟大或渺小，取决于他的意志力。

5. Nothing is impossible; the word itself says 'I'm possible'!
万事皆有可能，“不可能”的意思是“不，可能。”

6. Put your heart, mind, and soul into even your smallest acts. This is the secret of success.
即便是再微小不过的事情，你也要用心去做。这就是成功的秘密。

7. Give light and people will find the way.
照亮前方的路，路就会被找到。

8. Ideas shape the course of history.
想法改变了历史的进程。

读书笔记

28 On Making Friends 关于交友

Everyone needs friends, and if you fail to make friends, you should examine yourself and see if there is something wrong with your **personality**.

人人都需要朋友，若你在交朋友方面总是失败，就该反省自己，看是否你的性格有什么问题。

May be you have social faults such as **snobbishness**, **talkativeness** and using slang etc., which drive away your new **acquaintances**. Whatever your social faults may be, look at them honestly and make real effort to correct them.

或许你有些在社交上应该避讳的缺点，比如势力、饶舌、说脏话等，这些都会妨碍你结交新朋友。无论你有什么社交缺点，都该正视它们，尽力摒弃。

To be friendly you must feel friendly. Cheerfulness is the basis of friendliness. A **cheerful** people smiles. A smile is a **magnet** which draws people. Smile at someone and you are almost sure to get a smile in return.

要友善，你一定要给人友好的感觉：快乐是友善的基础。一个快乐的人总会面带微笑。微笑就像有吸引力的磁铁，你对别人微笑，你也会得到他微笑的回应。

A friendly person does his best to make a stranger feel at home, wherever he happens to be. Put yourself in the other fellow's place and make them feel welcome.

无论在哪里，友善之人都会让陌生人有自在舒适的感觉，设身处地为陌生人考虑，让他有备受欢迎的感觉。

Try to remember names. It makes your new acquaintances feel happy when you call them by their names. It gives them the feeling that they have made an **impression** on you and that mean something to them because you remember them.

尽量记住人名。对新认识的朋友直呼其名会令他们很高兴，他们会觉得你对他有了一定的印象，这说明你记住了他们，这对他们很重要。

If you don't agree with other people on a certain matter, you should appear to be friendly. Don't **argue**, but discuss. You always lose friends if you argue too much.

若在某件事上你不能与别人达成一致意见，你该表现出友好。可以讨论，但不要争吵。争吵过甚会使你失去朋友。

A friendly person thinks of others, and doesn't insist on his own "rights". People who refuse to consider others have few friends.

友善之人常为他人考虑，不会为自己争取"权利"。不顾及别人的人，他的朋友寥寥无几。

Finally, don't treat people only according to their social positions. Really friendly people respect everyone at all times.

最后，切勿以社会地位论人。真正的友善之人往往尊重别人。

单词解析 *Word Analysis*

personality [ˌpɜːsəˈnæləti] *n.* 个性，性格

例 She has such a kind, friendly personality.
她个性善良友好。

snobbishness [ˈsnɒbɪʃnəs] *n.* 过分自傲，势利

例 Their snobbishness made them dislike their intellectual and social inferiors.
他们非常势利，不喜欢智力和社会地位不如自己的人。

talkativeness [ˈtɔːkətɪvnɪs] *n.* 爱说话，饶舌

例 He had been inclined to talkativeness, but gradually he became rather reserved.
他过去是比较爱说话的，但慢慢变得沉默寡言了。

acquaintance [əkˈweɪntəns] *n.* 认识的人，泛泛之交

例 I have a large circle of friends and acquaintances engaged in photography.
我在摄影界交游甚广。

cheerful ['tʃɪəfl] *adj.* 欢快的，高兴的

例 Jack sounded quite cheerful about the idea.
杰克好像对这个想法很高兴。

magnet ['mægnət] *n.* 有吸引力的事物

例 Lower interest rates are acting like a magnet, dragging consumers back to the shops.
较低利率像磁铁一样吸引顾客又回到了商店。

impression [ɪm'preʃn] *n.* 印象，感想

例 My impression is that they are totally out of control.
我的感觉是它们完全失去了控制。

argue ['ɑːgjuː] *v.* 争吵，争辩

例 They were still arguing; I could hear them down the road.
他们还在争吵；我在马路的那头都能听见他们的声音。

语法知识点 *Grammar Points*

① Smile at someone and you are almost sure to get a smile in return.

in return 作为报答，反过来

例 These are gestures of genuine friendship with no favours expected in return.
这些都是真挚友谊的表示，并不期待任何回报。

类似词组in return for 作为……的回报

例 He bought a gift in return for her help.
他买了一个礼物，是作为对她帮助的回报。

② A friendly person does his best to make a stranger feel at home, wherever he happens to be.

do one's best to do sth. 尽某人最大努力做某事，相当于try one's best to do sth.

例 In one word, we must try our best to do the job.
总而言之，我们必须尽力去做这项工作。

happen to 碰巧，恰巧

例 If you happen to see Jane, ask her to phone me.
如果你凑巧见到简，叫她给我打个电话。

例 We learned what might happen to a world after a full-scale thermonuclear war.
我们了解了一旦爆发大规模热核战争，世界会成什么样子。

③ A friendly person thinks of others, and doesn't insist on his own "rights".

think of 考虑到，想到

例 I'm primarily thinking of the first year.
我考虑的主要是第一年。

insist on 坚持，强调

例 They are purists who insist on doing everything just as it has been done for centuries.
他们是纯粹主义者，坚持所有事情都要按照几百年来的方式去做。

以上insist是做不及物动词，后面跟on的用法，insist也可做及物动词，接从句做宾语，作"坚决要求" "一定要"讲，其宾语从句常用与将来事实相反的虚拟语气，即"should+动词原形"，其中should可以省略。

例 He insisted that we (should) accept these gifts.
他一定要我们收下这些礼物。

经典名句 *Famous Classics*

1. You must learn a new way to think before you can master a new way to be.
在掌握新方法之前，你必须要先换一种思考方法。

2. All we need is the awareness of how blessed we really are.
我们需要的只是意识到自己有多幸运。

3. If you are unhappy with anything—whatever is bringing you down—get rid of it. Because you will find that when you are free, your true creativity, your true self comes out.

如果你因某件事不开心，不管是什么，都不要去管它。因为你会发现当你不去想它的时候，你才能发挥出自己真正的创造力、才能做真正的自己。

4. To do the useful thing, to say the courageous thing, to contemplate the beautiful thing: that's enough for one man's life.
做有用的事，说勇敢的话，想美好的事，一生足矣。

5. A lot of people resist transition and therefore never allow themselves to enjoy who they are. Embrace the change, no matter what it is; once you do, you can learn about the new world you're in and take advantage of it.
很多人不愿改变，因此就失去了认识自己的机会。不管是什么改变，放开怀抱接受吧。一旦你做出改变，你就能更好地认识和利用你的新世界了。

读书笔记

29 On Friendship 论友谊

It had been hard for him that spake it to have put more truth and untruth together in few words, than in that speech, Whatsoever is delighted in solitude, is either a wild beast or a god. For it is most true, that a natural and secret hatred, and aversation towards society, in any man, hath somewhat of the savage beast; but it is most untrue, that it should have any character at all, of the divine nature; except it proceed, not out of a pleasure in solitude, but out of a love and desire to **sequester** a man's self, for a higher conversation: such as is found to have been falsely and feignedly in some of the heathen; as Epimenides the Canadian, Numa the Roman, Empedocles the Sicilian, and Apollonius of Tyana; and truly and really, in divers of the ancient hermits and holy fathers of the church. But little do men perceive what solitude is, and how far it extendeth. For a crowd is not company; and faces are but a gallery of pictures; and talk but a tinkling cymbal, where there is no love. The Latin adage meeteth with it a little: Magna civitas, magna solitudo; because in a great town friends are scattered; so that there is not

"喜欢孤独的人不是野兽便是神灵"。说这话的人若要在寥寥数语之中，更能把真理和邪说放在一处，那就很难了。因为，若说一个人心里有了一种天生的、隐秘的、对社会的憎恨嫌弃，则那个人不免带点野兽的性质，这是极其真实的；然而要说这样的一个人居然有任何神灵的性质，则是极不真实的。只有一点可为例外，那就是当这种憎恨社会的心理不是出于对孤独的爱好而是出于一种想把自己退出社会以求更崇高的生活的心理的时候；这样的人异教徒中有些人曾冒充过，如克瑞蒂人埃辟曼尼底斯、罗马人努马、西西利人安辟道克利斯和蒂安那人阿波郎尼亚斯是也；而基督教会中许多的古隐者和长老则确有如此者。但是一般人并不大明白何为孤独以及孤独的范围。因为在没有"仁爱"的地方，一群人并不能算作一个团体，许多的面目也仅仅是一列图画；而交谈则不过是铙钹丁令作声而已。这种情形有句拉丁成语略能形容之："一座大城市就是一片大荒野"；因为在一座大城市

that **fellowship**, for the most part, which is in less neighborhoods. But we may go further, and affirm most truly, that it is a mere and miserable **solitude** to want true friends; without which the world is but a **wilderness**; and even in this sense also of solitude, whosoever in the frame of his nature and **affections**, is unfit for friendship, he taketh it of the beast, and not from humanity.

A principal fruit of friendship, is the ease and discharge of the fullness and swellings of the heart, which passions of all kinds do cause and **induce**. We know diseases of stoppings, and **suffocations**, are the most dangerous in the body; and it is not much otherwise in the mind; you may take sarza to open the liver, steel to open the spleen, flowers of sulphur for the lungs, castoreum for the brain; but no receipt openeth the heart, but a true friend; to whom you may impart grieves, joys, fears, hopes, **suspicions**, counsels, and whatsoever lieth upon the heart to oppress it, in a kind of civil shrift or **confession.**

里朋友们是散居各处的，所以就其大概而言，不像在小一点的城镇里，有那样的交情。但是我们不妨更进一步并且很真实地断言说，缺乏真正的朋友乃是最纯粹最可怜的孤独；没有友谊则斯世不过是一片荒野；我们还可以用这个意义来论“孤独”说，凡是天性不配交友的人其性情可说是来自禽兽而不是来自人类。

友谊的主要效用之一就在使人心中的愤懑抑郁之气得以宣泄弛放，这些不平之气是各种情感都可以引起的。闭塞之症于人的身体最为凶险，这是我们知道的；在人的精神方面亦复如此：你可以服撒尔沙以通肝，服钢以通脾，服硫华以通肺，服海狸胶以通脑，然而除了一个真心的朋友之外没有一样药剂是可以通心的。对一个真心的朋友你可以传达你的忧愁、欢悦、恐惧、希望、疑忌、谏言，以及任何压在你心上的事情，有如一种教堂以外的忏悔一样。

单词解析 Word Analysis

sequester [sɪ'kwestə(r)] v. 使隔绝，使隔离

例 This jury is expected to be sequestered for at least two months.
预计这个陪审团将至少被隔离两个月。

fellowship ['feləʊʃɪp] *n.* 团体，协会

例 At Merlin's instigation, Arthur founds the Fellowship of the Round Table.

在梅林的建议下，亚瑟王创建了圆桌骑士团。

solitude ['sɒlɪtjuːd] *n.* 独居，独处

例 He enjoyed his moments of solitude before the pressures of the day began.

他喜欢在白天的压力到来之前享受独处的时光。

wilderness ['wɪldənəs] *n.* 荒野，荒漠

例 He is proud of the garden he made from a wilderness.

他为自己从荒地上开辟出的花园而感到自豪。

affection [ə'fekʃn] *n.* 喜爱，钟爱

例 She had developed quite an affection for the place.

她逐渐对这个地方钟爱有加。

induce [ɪn'djuːs] *v.* 引起，导致

例 Doctors said surgery could induce a heart attack.

医生们说手术有可能引起心脏病发作。

suffocation [ˌsʌfə'keɪʃn] *n.* 窒息

例 Many of the victims died of suffocation.

许多遇难者是窒息死亡的。

suspicion [sə'spɪʃn] *n.* 怀疑，疑心

例 He may have had some suspicions of Michael Foster, the editor of the journal.

他可能对杂志主编迈克尔·福斯特有些怀疑。

confession [kən'feʃn] *n.* 承认，坦白

例 The diaries are a mixture of confession and observation.

这些日记既有自白，也有评论。

语法知识点 *Grammar Points*

① Whatsoever is delighted in solitude, is either a wild beast or a god.

either…or 表示选择，连接句中两个并列成分，其意为“要么……要么……”“或者……或者……”

例 The clock is available with either Roman or Arabic numerals.
这款钟有带罗马数字的，也有带阿拉伯数字的。

使用either...or...时还应注意，连接两个成分作主语时，谓语动词通常与其靠近的主语保持一致。

例 Either you or I am going there tomorrow.
明天要么你去那里，要么我去那里。

如果把上句变成一般疑问句，助动词形式与主语you保持一致，所以要用are提问，而不是am。

例 Are either you or I going there tomorrow?
明天是你还是我去那里?

② …it should have any character at all, of the divine nature; except it proceed, not out of a pleasure in solitude…

out of 短语介词，意思很多，用法颇为复杂，上句表示“出于……动机”“由于……原因”

例 The traffic accident was out of carelessness in driving.
这起交通事故是由于粗心驾驶所致。

out of 基本用法可表示地点“从里向外”

例 This animal is not found out of certain areas in Africa.
这种动物只在非洲某些地区有。

表示竭尽和缺乏

例 We are out of tea.
我们的茶叶用完了。

表示材料或者来源

例 This paragraph is out of Marx's works in the original.
这一段引自马克思原著。

经典名句 *Famous Classics*

1. There are two ways of spreading light: to be the candle or the mirror that reflects it.
传递光亮有两种方式：成为一支蜡烛或当一面镜子。

2. Making the absolute best of ourselves is not an easy task. It is a pleasurable pursuit...but it requires patience, persistence, and perseverance.
做最好的自己并不容易，这是很美好的愿望，需要耐心、坚持和毅力。

3. If you don't enjoy your life, sorrow, sadness, fear, shame and guilt will.
如果你不好好享受生活，你的悲伤、难过、害怕、羞愧和内疚会代替你享受。

4. We can never give up wishing while we are thoroughly alive. There are certain things we feel to be beautiful and good, and we must hunger after them.
我们从不应该在活着的时候放弃希望。我们会为一些事而感到美好，而这些事是我们必须自己去追寻的。

5. Whatever I believed, I did; and whatever I did, I did with my whole heart and mind.
凡是我相信的，我都做了；凡是我做了的事，都是全身心地投入去做的。

6. If you wish to succeed, you should use persistence as your good friend, experience as your reference, prudence as your brother and hope as your sentry.
如果你希望成功，当以恒心为良友、以经验为参谋、以谨慎为兄弟、以希望为哨兵。

7. Never be unduly elated by victory or depressed by defeat.
胜不骄，败不馁。

8. Only those who have the patience to do simple things perfectly ever acquire the skill to do difficult things easily.
只有有耐心圆满完成简单工作的人，才能够轻而易举地完成困难的事。

30 My Old Penholder
笔杆，我的老伙伴

For more than a week my pen has lain untouched. I have written nothing for seven whole days, not even a letter. Except during one or two bouts of illness, such a thing never happened in my life before. In my life; the life, that is, which had to be supported by anxious toil; the life which was not lived for living's sake, as all life should be, but under the goad of fear. The **earning** of money should be a means to an end; for more than thirty years I began to support myself at sixteen and had to regard it as the end itself.

I could imagine that my old **penholder** feels **reproachfully** towards me. Has it not served me well? Why do I, in my happiness, let it lie there neglected, gathering dust? The same penholder that has lain against my **forefinger** day after day, for how many years? Twenty, at least; I remember buying it at a shop in Tottenham Court Road. By the same token I bought that day a paperweight, which cost me a whole shilling—an extravagance which made me tremble. The penholder shone with its new varnish, now it is plain brown wood

我的笔已经个把星期躺在那里没人碰它。整整七天我什么也没有写，连一封信也没有写。有生以来除了一两次生病期间，从来不曾有过这样的事。我这一生是全靠兢兢业业艰苦劳动来维持生活的，这一生不是为了生活而生活，像所有生活应该有的情况那样，而是在恐惧下挣扎苟活的一生。挣钱本不是生活的目的，而不过是达到目的的手段。我从十六岁起独自谋生，三十多年以来我却不得不把挣钱当作目的。

我可以想象，我的老伙伴笔杆在责备我。它不是很好地为我服务过了吗？为什么我在幸福之中把它弃置不度，让它躺在那里沾灰呢？正是这支笔杆日复一日地依着我的食指，已经有多少年了？至少二十年，我记得是在托特纳姆广场路一家铺子里买的。既买了笔，那天我就又买了一只镇纸，这使我花费了整整一个先令——这种浪费当时叫我发抖。刚买时，笔杆是油光铮亮的，现在从头到尾都只剩棕色

from end to end. On my forefinger it has made a **callosity.**

Old companion, yet old enemy! How many a time have I taken it up, loathing the necessity, heavy in head and heart? My hand shaking, my eyes sick-dazzled. How I dreaded the white page I had to foul with ink ! Above all, on days scub as this, when the blue eyes of Spring, laughed from between rosy clouds, when the sunlight shimmered upon my table and made me long, long all but to madness, for the scent of the flowering earth, for the green of hillside larches, for the singing of the **skylark** above the downs. There was a time that it seems further away than childhood when I hook up my pen with **eagerness**; if my hand trembled it was with hope. But a hope that fooled me, for never a page of my writing deserved to live. I can say that now without **bitterness**. It was youthful error, and only the force of circumstance prolonged it. The world has done me no **injustice**; thank Heaven I have grown wise enough not to rail at it for this; And why should any man who writes, even if he write things immortal, nurse anger at the world's neglect? Who asked him to publish? Who promised him a hearing? Who has broken faith with him? If my shoemaker turn me out an excellent pair of boots, and I, in some

的木质本色了。这笔杆曾叫我的食指磨出老茧。

我的老伙伴，可又是我的老对头！有多少次我拿起这笔杆，头脑昏沉沉，心里沉甸甸、手发抖，眼发花，感到厌恶而不得不写。看到不得不用墨水来涂污的白纸，我真害怕。尤其是碰上这样的日子——当春天的蓝湛湛的眼睛从玫瑰色的云缝里欢笑，当阳光在我的书桌上闪烁，使我几乎发狂地想念那百花盛开的大地的芳馨，想念那山坡上落叶松的一片青翠，思念那丘陵上空云雀的歌声时，我更是害怕了。想当年——仿佛比童年还早些——每当提笔，我总是充满热望。那时如果我的手发抖，那是为希望而发抖。可是希望作弄了我，因为我的文章没有一页值得保存。现在我能说这话而不感到心酸了。那是我年轻时犯下的错误，由于环境所迫，才延误至今。这世界并没有对我不公平。感谢上苍，我现已知事明理，不会为此错误怨天尤人了。一个人写了点东西，哪怕是写出了不朽的作品，何必因未受世人的重视而怀恨在心呢？谁要他出版的？谁向他保证过必有人听他的？又是谁违背信念？如果我的鞋匠给我一双漂亮靴子，正

mood of cantankerous unreason, throw them back upon his hands, the man has just cause of complaint. But your poem, your novel, who bargained with you for it? If it is honest journeywork, yet lacks purchasers, at most you may call yourself a hapless tradesman. If it come from on high, with what **decency** do you fret and fume because it is not paid for in heavy cash? For the work of man's mind there is one test, and one alone, the judgment of generations yet unborn. If you have written a great book, the world to come will know of it. But you don't care for posthumous glory. You want to enjoy fame in a comfortable armchair. Ah, that is quite another thing. Have the courage of your desire. Admit yourself a merchant, and protest to gods and men that the merchandise you offer is of better quality than much which sells for a high price. You may be right, and indeed it is hard upon you that fashion does not turn to your stall.

遇上我心情不好，蛮不讲理，把靴子扔回他手里，那鞋匠就有正当理由来抱怨。可是你的诗，你的小说，谁跟你谈好这笔生意了？如果那是一件货真价实的商品，可是没有买主，你至多只能说你自己是个不走运的店主。如果那是凭空来的，你有什么脸面由于它没有人高价买它而烦恼和光火呢？对于人的心灵的产品，只有——也只能有一种检验，那就是未来的一代一代人的评判。如果你果真写出了一部伟大的作品，未来的世界会知道它的。偏偏你不爱身后的光荣，你要舒舒服服坐在安乐椅里享受盛名，嗯，这就完全是另一回事了。那么你就勇敢地提出你的要求吧，你得承认你是个商人，并对神和人声明，说你提供的货色比许多卖高价的质量更高。说不定你是对的，而倘若时髦人物还是不肯光顾你的货摊，那就真是使你极其难受了。

单词解析 *Word Analysis*

earning [ˈɜːnɪŋ] *n.* 收入，赚取的钱

例 He was a high-earning broker with money to burn.
他是高收入的经纪人，有花不完的钱。

penholder ['pen,həʊldə] *n.* 笔插，笔架

例 I want to make a penholder with this bamboo.

我要用这根竹子做成一个笔筒。

reproachfully [rɪ'prəʊtʃfəlɪ] *adv.* 责备地

例 Jack's mother stopped smiling and looked reproachfully at him.

杰克的妈妈收起了笑容，用责备的眼光看着他。

forefinger ['fɔːfɪŋgə(r)] *n.* 食指

例 He took the pen between his thumb and forefinger.

他用拇指和食指捏着笔。

callosity [kæ'lɒsɪtɪ] *n.* 无情，冷酷

例 However, people sometimes are hurt by callosity.

然而，有时人们总被无情伤。

skylark ['skaɪlɑːk] *n.* 云雀

例 Shelley called the skylark a "blithe spirit" because of its happy song.

雪莱把云雀称作是"欢乐的精灵"，因为它的歌声令人陶醉。

eagerness ['iːgənɪs] *n.* 热切，渴望

例 His hands trembled with eagerness as he opened the letter.

他拆信时因急切而双手发抖。

bitterness ['bɪtənəs] *n.* 苦味，痛苦，悲痛

例 There was a strain of bitterness in his voice.

他的声音听起来有些愤愤不平。

injustice [ɪn'dʒʌstɪs] *n.* 不公平，非正义

例 They resented the injustices of the system.

他们怨恨制度的种种不公。

decency ['diːsnsi] *n.* 正派，合宜，得体

例 Unfortunately, on Friday night he showed neither decency nor dignity.

不幸的是，周五晚上他表现得既不得体，也不庄重。

语法知识点 *Grammar Points*

① …the life which was not lived for living's sake, as all life should be, but under the goad of fear.

for living's sake 为了活着

for...sake，为了，由于，看在……份上，相当于for the sake of。

例 But Moses replied, "Are you jealous for my sake?"
摩西对他说："你为我的缘故嫉妒人吗？"

例 They roped her on to us for the sake of safety.
安全起见，他们用绳子把她和我们相互系在一起。

② By the same token I bought that day a paperweight, which cost me a whole shilling, an extravagance which made me tremble.

by the same token 出于同样的原因

例 The two workers were dismissed from the factory by the same token.
那两位工人以同样的方式被工厂解雇了。

例 By the same token, it would be pointless to live in sickness.
同样地，生活在病痛中也是无意义的。

经典名句 *Famous Classics*

1. People often ask me if I know the secret of success, and if I could tell others how to make their dreams come true. My answer is, do it by working.
人们时常问我是否晓得成功的诀窍，能否告诉别人怎样使他们的梦想成为现实。我的回答是：身体力行。

2. Power invariably means both responsibility and danger.
实力永远意味着责任和危险。

3. We are absolutely different persons. This individual distinction

may cause conflict between us is every aspect of our life. Don't immerse ourselves in this infliction too long.
我们是完全不同的个体。这种个体差异可能会在生活的方方面面给我们带来冲突。不要让自己过多地沉浸在这种伤害之中。

4. Silence is the element in which great things fashion themselves.
沉默是造就伟大速写的因素。

5. Friendship takes a special kind of love that seems to know no end. Never hesitate to show your heartfelt care and kindness to your friend when he/she is in trouble.
结交朋友需要具备一种特殊的似乎无止境的爱。当他/她处于困境时，永远不要犹豫，而要向你的朋友表示出由衷的关怀和善意。

读书笔记

31 To Cherish Friends 珍惜朋友

The old bell was ringing calling us to breakfast at the camp.

夏令营的营地里，一只老旧的摇铃响个不停，招呼我们该吃早饭了。

Several of us, however, weren't paying attention.

可是，我们中的好几个人根本不去理会。

It was the last day of camp and we were engaging in a tradition passed down for years.

这是夏令营的最后一天，我们正在举行一场数年来沿袭下来的传统仪式。

We were supposed to have stripped the sheets off of our beds in our cabins, **stuff** them into our pillow cases, and return them to the office before breakfast.

我们本应把宿舍里床上的床单扯下来，把他们塞进枕套里，在早餐之前把他们归还到办公室去。

Pillow cases filled with heavy sheets, though, were far better than pillows for an end of the week pillow fight.

可是，塞进厚床单的枕套比枕头要好得多，很适合来一场宿营最后一天的枕头大战。

A dozen or more of us then were going at it when the bell started to ring.

铃声响起的时候，包括我在内的十几个学员正在激烈对战。

We were knocking each other over the beds and swinging our loaded down pillow cases with all of our might.

我们把对方从床上打到地上去，用我们全身的力气挥舞着手中塞得满满的枕套。

A hit to the head stung like crazy but we didn't mind.

脑袋被砸得生疼，简直让人发疯，但我们毫不在意。

We were having a rough housing good time.

我们正在享受这番大闹宿舍的好时光。

Soon the pillow fight spilled out into the hallway of the second story of our cabin.

很快枕头大战的战场就扩散到了二楼大厅。

A friend of mine and I were getting the worst of it.

我和我的一个朋友打得最凶。

Several of the other boys had decided to gang up against us.

I swung at one of them and missed and then saw another pillow case coming straight at my head.

I ducked and it caught my friend full in the chest.

Unfortunately, he was standing at the **edge** of the narrow **stairway** that led to the second floor.

I looked around and saw that he was **airborne**, going backwards down the steps.

He seemed about to **crack** his head wide open on the wooden steps when someone stripping their sheets on the first floor let their mattress fall on the bottom of the steps.

My friend landed on the mattress and rolled safely off of it.

The pillow fight stopped cold as we all gazed in **amazement.**

"Whoa!," someone said. "What a lucky break!"

Looking back on that moment now I know that it wasn't just a lucky break.

So many of us these days focus on the times when something bad happens to us.

We fail to see all of the times when something bad could have happened to us and **miraculously** didn't.

I know that there are no **coincidences**

几个其他的男孩决定联合起来对付我们。

我朝他们中的一个发起攻击，没有打中，接着就看到一个枕套径直朝我的脑袋飞过来。

我躲开了，我的朋友却正好被砸中了胸口。

不幸的是，他正好站在通往二楼的狭窄楼梯的拐角处。

我转过头去，发现他四脚腾空，朝楼梯下面倒去。

眼看他就要在木头阶梯上摔个脑袋开花，突然，一个正在一楼拆床单的人把床垫放在楼梯底部。

我的朋友摔进了床垫里，打了个滚，安全无恙。

我们目瞪口呆地看着这一切，枕头大战戛然而止。

"哇！"有人叫到，"真是太走运啦！"

现在再回想那个时刻，我知道这不单单是运气。

如今我们中许多人只会去注意那些坏事情真的降临的时候。

我们没有发现，那么多次，某件坏事本会发生，却奇迹般的没有发生。

我知道生命中本没有纯粹的巧合。

我们都被他人照看着，我们都被保护着，我们都被爱着。

当你"走运"时，好好珍

in this life.

We are all watched over. We are all guided. We are all loved.

Use your "lucky breaks" here well then.

Don't waste a second of this precious time you are given.

Live! Learn! Love! This life here is gift to you. Make how you live it your gift to others.

惜吧！

生命给予我们的时间是珍贵的，不要浪费一分一秒！

认真生活，学习新知，关爱他人吧！让你认真生活的态度成为对他人的礼物！

单词解析 Word Analysis

stuff [stʌf] *v.* 把……塞进(或填进)

例 He stuffed the newspapers into a litter bin and headed down the street.

他把报纸塞进了垃圾箱，然后沿街往前走了。

edge [edʒ] *n.* 边缘

例 We were on a hill, right on the edge of town.

我们在恰位于城镇边缘的一座小山上。

stairway ['steəweɪ] *n.* 楼梯，阶梯

例 The stone stairway was covered with lichen.

那石级长满了地衣。

airborne ['eəbɔːn] *adj.* 空气中的，空气中传播的

例 Many people are allergic to airborne pollutants such as pollen.

许多人对空气传播的污染物过敏，比如花粉。

crack [kræk] *v.* 破裂，使断裂

例 A gas main cracked under his garage and gas seeped into our homes.

他家车库下面的煤气总管裂开了，煤气渗入了我们家。

amazement [ə'meɪzmənt] *n.* 惊讶，惊愕

例 I stared at her in amazement.
我惊愕地瞪眼看着她。

miraculously [mɪ'rækjələslɪ] *adv.* 奇迹般地

例 It was a terrible explosion but, miraculously, no one was killed.
这是一次可怕的爆炸，但是没有一个人死亡，真是奇迹。

coincidence [kəʊ'ɪnsɪdəns] *n.* 一致，巧合

例 He said the timing was a coincidence and that his decision was unrelated to Mr. Roman's departure.
他说这是时间上的巧合，他的决定与罗曼先生的离开没有关系。

语法知识点 *Grammar Points*

① It was the last day of camp and we were engaging in a tradition passed down for years.

engage in 参与，从事，用于肯定语气中，多表达的是“主动地参与”

例 Companies shall engage in business activities within their registered scope of business.
公司应当在登记的经营范围内从事经营活动。

be engaged in 忙于，相当于be busy doing sth.

passed down for years 做后置定语，修饰前面的tradition，原型为pass down，译为“流传下来”。

例 This is a folk story passed down by the Jewish people.
这是一则犹太人流传下来的民间故事。

② We were supposed to have stripped the sheets off of our beds in our cabins.

be supposed to do 意为“应该、被期望、理应”，用来表示根据规定或传统习惯人们不得不做的事。时态、人称和句式的变化用be来体现，to为不定式符号，后接动词原形。

例 Everyone is supposed to wear a seat-belt in the car.
每个人在小汽车里都应该系好安全带。

例 Was Lucy supposed to speak Chinese like that?
露西应该像那样说汉语吗?

例 You are not supposed to smoke here.
你不应该在这里抽烟。

suppose作动词，意为“认为、猜想、想象”，suppose的后面接从句或to be作宾语。

例 We all suppose Jenny to be the best student in our class.
我们都认为珍妮是我们班里最好的学生。

经典名句 *Famous Classics*

1. All endings are beginnings; we just don't know it at the time.
所有的结局都是新的开始，只是当时不知道。

2. Someday you will understand, you were the first to love yourself.
总有一天你会明白，人首先要爱自己。

3. We've gone through so much but eventually we come back to where we were.
我们经过那么多考验，最后还是回到了原点。

4. Promise more, not to be; that is just a lie.
承诺再多，做不到，那也只不过还是谎言。

5. If you hate me, I don't really care. I don't live to please you.
如果你讨厌我，我一点也不介意。我活着不是为了取悦你。

6. If you don't live for something, you'll die for nothing.
活着无所追求，至死都会一无所有。

读书笔记

32 Friendship between Men
男人间的友谊

The silence of men in general is overtalked about and over **criticized.** To be sure, men never open up as much as women want them to, but there is a **wordless** understanding in which we function fairly well especially in friendships.

男人的沉默往往被过多地谈论且过分指责。但可以肯定的是，男人从未像女人所希望的那样开诚布公地说出自己的心里话，但我们却能很好地运用无言的理解，尤其是在维持彼此的友谊的过程中。

I believe, in fact, that most women would prefer a man to be glumly uncommunicative than to spill his guts at the drop of a hat.

事实上，我相信大多数女人都宁愿男人可以忧郁地不言不语，而不喜欢男人就像竹筒倒豆子，什么都说。

The push for men to express their feelings **presumes** that we have feelings, and we do have a few, but they remain **submerged,** and the airing of them often **violates** their authenticity.

男人被认定为应表达感情，这就是他们表达情感的推动力。不错，我们确实有一些，但隐而不露，若要表达出来就会破坏其真实性。

I am no biologist, but my guess is that the male human animal was programmed for silence. I would go so far as to argue that men were programmed to be isolated from one another and that **aloneness** is our natural state. Silence in male friendships is our way of being alone with each other.

我不是生物学家，但我猜想男人这种动物天生就是沉默寡言的。我甚至认为男人天生就是彼此孤立的，孤独是我们的自然状态。男人间的友谊表现为沉默寡言，正是我们彼此独自生活方式的表现。

Once men have established a friendship, that itself is the word. The affection is obvious, at least to us. A main **component** of our silence is an **appreciation** of the **obvious**.

一旦男人间建立起友谊，友谊本身就已说明了一切。情感是明显的，至少对我们来说，我们沉默的一个主要组成部分就是对这明显情感的欣赏。

单词解析 Word Analysis

criticize ['krɪtɪsaɪz] *v.* 批评，指责，批判

例 His mother had rarely criticized him or any of her children.
他母亲很少指责他或她的任何孩子。

wordless ['wɜːdləs] *adj.* 无言的，沉默的

例 Here and there, husbands sit in wordless despair.
丈夫们各处坐着，默默无言，绝望至极。

presume [prɪ'zjuːm] *v.* 假设，假定

例 The legal definition of "know" often presumes mental control.
"知晓"的法律定义通常假定存在思维控制能力。

submerge [səb'mɜːdʒ] *v.* （使）淹没，（使）浸没

例 The river burst its banks, submerging an entire village.
河水决堤，淹没了整个村庄。

violate ['vaɪəleɪt] *v.* 违反，违背

例 They violated the ceasefire agreement.
他们违反了停火协议。

aloneness [ə'ləʊnɪs] *n.* 孤独感

例 Celebrate being alone, delight in yourself, and dance in your aloneness.
为孤独庆祝，为自己高兴，为你的孤独舞蹈。

component [kəm'pəʊnənt] *n.* 组成部分

例 The management plan has four main components.
管理计划有4个主要部分。

appreciation [əˌpriːʃi'eɪʃn] *n.* 欣赏，赏识

例 Brian whistled in appreciation.
布赖恩吹口哨以示赞赏。

obvious ['ɒbviəs] *adj.* 明显的，显著的

例 It's obvious that you need more time to think.

显然你需要更多时间来思考。

语法知识点 *Grammar Points*

① I believe, in fact, that most women would prefer a man to be glumly uncommunicative than to spill his guts at the drop of a hat.

in fact 实际上，相当于actually。actually可以修饰动词、形容词以及副词。

例 In fact, we were innocent of the crime.
事实上，我们是无辜的。

例 Some patients actually got worse after receiving the treatment.
有些病人在接受治疗后，病情事实上反而严重了。

prefer的用法很多，具体如下：
后接不定式时与rather than 或instead of 连用。

例 He preferred to die rather than (to) steal.
他宁死也不去偷窃。

prefer＋名词或动名词“宁愿”“更喜欢”

例 He comes from Shanghai, so he prefers rice.
他是上海人，因此更喜欢吃米饭。

prefer (sb.) to do “愿意（某人）做”

例 I prefer you to go at once.
我倒希望你马上就走。

prefer to do sth. rather than do sth. “宁愿做……而不做……”

例 I prefer to watch TV rather than go out.
我宁愿看电视也不出去。

prefer＋ **that** 从句“宁愿”（从句一般用虚拟语气）

例 I prefer that you should do it.
我宁愿你做这件事。

at the drop of a hat 美国习惯用语，字面意思是“帽子一旦落地”，这实际上也是一个信号的意思。也就是说，一有信号就马上行动。它现在多用来指一个脾气一触即发的人。

例 Say something he doesn't agree with, and he'll start a loud argument at the drop of a hat.

谁要是说一些和他意见不同的话，他可以马上大声嚷嚷，跟人家争辩。

② I would go so far as to argue that men were programmed...

go so far as to 甚至，竟然到了……地步

例 I won't go so far as to say that he is dishonest.

我不至于说他不诚实。

经典名句 *Famous Classics*

1. Everything stays the same; I just can't do it.
一切没有改变，只是我已无能为力。

2. I will learn to give up you, because I love you.
我会学着放弃你，因为我爱你。

3. Being hurt by the truth is better than comforted by the lies.
被真相伤害，总比被谎言安慰要好。

4. Life is really simple, but we insist on making it complicated.
生活一直都很简单，但是我们也一直都忍不住要把它变得很复杂。

5. Never regret something that once made you smile.
不必遗憾，至少她曾让你微笑。

6. To me, the past is black and white, but the future is always colorful.
对我而言，过去平淡无奇；而未来，却是绚烂缤纷。

读书笔记